DOUBLE WINNERS OF THE MEDAL OF HONOR

by
Dr. Ray Tassin

Daring Books
Canton • Ohio

DEDICATION

DEDICATED TO the Boone, Bordelon, David, DuCote, Lollis, Petty, St. Romain and Tassin branches of my family who — for eight consecutive generations — have fought America's wars.

Copyright © 1986 by
Dr. Ray Tassin

All rights reserved.

Published by Daring Books
P.O. Box 526 D, Canton, Ohio 44701

Library of Congress Cataloging-in-Publication Data

Tassin, Ray.
    Double winners of the medal of honor.

  1. Medal of Honor. 2. United States--Armed Forces--Biography. I. Title.
UB433.T37 1986   355.1'342'0922 [B]   86-6198
ISBN 0-938936-42-5

Printed in the United States of America.

TABLE OF CONTENTS

                                            Page

Chapter One 7
    Thomas Ward Custer — 3 April, 6 April 1865, Virginia.

Chapter Two 42
    John Cooper — 5 August 1864, 26 April 1865, Mobile Bay, Alabama.

Chapter Three...............................52
    Patrick Mullen — 17 March 1865, Mattox Creek, Virginia; 1 May 1865, at sea.

Chapter Four................................60
    Frank Baldwin — 20 July 1864, Georgia; 8 November 1874, Texas.

Chapter Five 85
    Patrick Leonard — 15 May 1870, 28 April 1876, Nebraska.

Chapter Six 93
    William Wilson — 28 March 1872, 29 September 1872, Texas.

Chapter Seven..............................103
    Albert Weisbogel — 11 January 1874, 27 April 1876, at sea.

Chapter Eight 107
    Henry Hogan — October 1876-January 1877,
    30 September 1877, Montana.

Chapter Nine 116
    Robert Sweeney — 26 October 1881, Hampton
    Road, Virginia; 20 December 1883, New York.

Chapter Ten 123
    Louis Williams — 16 March 1883, Honolulu,
    Hawaii; 13 June 1884, Peru.

Chapter Eleven 127
    Daniel Joseph Daly — 14 August 1900, China;
    24 October 1915, Haiti.

Chapter Twelve 159
    John McCloy — 13, 20, 21, and 22 June 1900,
    China; 22 April 1914, Vera Cruz.

Chapter Thirteen 169
    Smedley D. Butler — 22 April 1914, Vera Cruz;
    17 November 1915, Haiti.

Chapter Fourteen 187
    John King — 29 May 1901, 13 September 1909,
    at sea.

Chapter Fifteen 198
    Ernest A. Janson — 6 June 1918, Chateau-
    Thierry (both awards).

Chapter Sixteen 202
    Matej Kocak — 18 July, 1918, Soissons (both
    awards).

Chapter Seventeen 209
   Louis Cukela — 18 July 1918, Soissons (both awards).

Chapter Eighteen 213
   John Henry Pruitt — 3 October 1918, Blanc Mont Ridge (both awards).

Chapter Nineteen 217
   John Joseph Kelly — 3 October 1918, Blanc Mont Ridge (both awards).

CHAPTER ONE

Thomas Ward Custer
(1845-76)

Civil War correspondents used the phrase "Custer's Luck" to describe the flamboyant Major General George Armstrong Custer. But the term applies as well to the General's younger brother, Thomas Ward Custer, who rode and died at his side and became the nation's first double winner of the Medal of Honor.

Tom's first bit of luck came soon after the outbreak of the Civil War. A team of army recruiters came to Monroe, Michigan, on a swing through the state organizing a regiment of Michigan cavalry. All the Custer boys were "born to horse." George Armstrong, the oldest at 22, was fresh out of West Point and already on duty with the cavalry in the Army of the Potomac. It surprised no one, then, when the three boys still living at home decided to enlist.

Nevin, 18, Tom, 16, and Boston, 14, cornered papa, old Emanuel, and told him of their plans. Papa said no. Armstrong was already following the guidon. That was contribution enough for one family. Besides, they were needed at home to tend the stock and farm the land.

But the boys didn't give up that easily, and papa likely didn't expect them to. They begged, badgered and bluffed until he agreed one of them could go if the other two would stay home with no further talk of enlisting.

The boys agreed. But which one would go?

The oldest, Nevin, got first choice, papa said. Nevin grinned while Tom and Boston bit back their disappointment. They wouldn't even go to the recruiting station with Nevin.

They should have gone, however. Nevin returned home crestfallen, rejected for service due to his generally sickly physical condition. Ironically, he would outlive all of his more hardy brothers.

Elated, Tom raced his horse into town. A fine physical specimen just like Armstrong, Tom knew he could pass the test. At the frame building used by the recruiters, he found a line of farm youths waiting to become Michigan cavalrymen. Not noted for his supply of patience, Tom nevertheless worked up through the line until he stood in front of the table where a clerk filled out papers under the watchful eye of the recruiting officer.

Name?

Thomas Ward Custer.

Age?

Uh, eighteen.

The recruiting officer interrupted at this point. He had it on good authority that this young man was only sixteen — too young for this outfit.

Tom exploded with all the reasons why his age shouldn't keep him out, but the officer adamantly refused to reconsider. If the war lasted two years, which wasn't likely, maybe Tom could try again.

Tom stomped out of the station, his ears burning from the laughter of the older men of 18 and 19.

Back home, Tom ranted to his brother. How did they know he was only sixteen? Who was the "good authority?" He sure looked older.

Papa told the recruiter his real age, Nevin said. He arranged for the rejection. Tom didn't confront papa over the matter, but he didn't give up that easily either. He had been born in nearby Ohio, in the hamlet of New Rumley, so he simply rode across the border 2 September 1861, and enlisted in the 21st Ohio Infantry.

And thus began the military career that would end fifteen years later when Tom and four other members of his family would die together on the Little Big Horn River in Montana.

Because of his youthful vigor and superb horsemanship, Tom became an aide to General James Scott Negley in the Army of Ohio. In the next three years, he matured in battles from Shiloh to Chickamauga. He even made corporal in the spring of 1864. Then "Custer's Luck" smiled on him again.

While Tom spent three years working up to corporal, Armstrong jumped in rank to brigadier general at the age of 23 — the youngest in history — more by reckless daring than unusual military ability. Now, in the fall of 1864, Armstrong used his considerable influence in the military to get Tom commissioned as a second lieutenant in the Sixth Michigan Cavalry and assigned him to his staff.

Troopers of the Sixth Michigan didn't think much of their newest lieutenant, due partly to his political appointment by his brother, the regimental commander, and partly to his former service in the walking army. But they tolerated him.

The brothers looked much alike by now. Each had long reddish golden hair, a whipcord body, humorous mouth, sharp nose and narrow blue eyes often sparkling with devilment.

Tom donned the red cravat that was the trademark of the Sixth Michigan and swaggered with the rest, only more so. He lived in Armstrong's house when not in the field during the winter of 1864. In public, the Custer brothers displayed the dignity expected of officers, but behind the closed doors of their home they romped about like school boys. Elizabeth (Libbie), Armstrong's wife, became a second mother to Tom — or perhaps a sister, for the three would bound around the house like children playing a noisy game of tag.

In November 1864, the regiment moved through the Shenandoah Valley destroying everything the Rebels might use for food and shelter.

The final spring campaign of the Civil War started for Sheridan's Cavalry of 9,000 on 27 February 1865, one of the few pleasant days of that rugged winter. Armstrong commanded 1,500 men, leading the division in search of General Jubal Early's Cavalry. The mild weather soon vanished, replaced by freezing rain. The trail became a quagmire of red Virginia mud. The column slipped, slid, staggered, sunk and sloshed on slowly.

As a staff officer, Tom relayed orders, ran errands, and helped keep the intervals closed up between troops. The mud, from knee deep to belly deep on the horses, held the march to only sixteen miles by noon 2 March as still the rain drenched the column. When the mud got too deep for riding, Tom struggled alongside his horse. He could barely see his uniform under the red slime. About noon, Armstrong summoned the staff up front, and Tom struggled forward to his brother's side.

Off to the left lay the scrubby village of Waynesboro, Virginia, half hidden by the rain. Along a ridge west of town was strung a line of dirt breastworks, overturned wagons and other makeshift defensive positions. It looked like a couple of brigades of infantry were manning the line, with a dozen or so artillery pieces and cavalry behind the line — about 2,000 seasoned fighters.

The fortifications stretched to the right downhill toward

the South River, but didn't actually reach all the way, leaving the left flank exposed. Armstrong decided to send one brigade against that soft spot while attacking the center with the main force. But his column was strung out for miles, still struggling with the mud. They could only fret and wait.

Tom paced his horse back and forth while the First Brigade slowly gathered. Though he felt a growing excitement, he had no way of knowing that this was destined to be one of five great moments in his life. His actions that day would set the pattern for his conduct in battle for the remaining eleven years of his life, but all he really understood was his impatience.

Finally the First Brigade struggled into position for the assault. Armstrong ordered an attack, without hope they could break through. A line of musket fire blazed out from the defensive line long before the horse soldiers reached it, halting its forward surge. Two additional brigades slowly formed into position, while the First Brigade retreated.

Armstrong next sent one brigade to circle around the left flank of the enemy while the other two brigades hammered at the line. Tom smarted under the expected failure, which may have influenced his actions in the next attack.

Likely Tom didn't plan it, but he led the charge against the center, galloping thirty yards out front and shouting with an exhilaration he didn't even understand at the time. Volley fire swept past him, but "Custer's Luck" kept him untouched while he leaped his horse over the breastworks. He fired his revolver into the gray-clad forms as he swept by. It was the type of exhibition that has inspired soldiers throughout time. It inspired the troopers to follow their brash lieutenant now.

Powder smoke soon swirled everywhere in the pounding rain, stinging the nostrils and obscuring Tom's vision but also affording him a measure of protection in his reckless charging about.

Tom emptied his revolver countless times in the liquid battle, and countless times rebel bullets snarled past him. As the defenders dropped back and regrouped, he pressed forward, with troopers who followed as naturally as if he had been their leader for years. He was the type of soldier who never considered the possibility that an enemy shot would ever do him serious harm. And for eleven more years he would be right in this assumption.

Meanwhile the brigade charging around the left flank broke through, rolling up the flank and weakening the entire line. Gradually the resistance weakened, and it died out after three hours. General Early escaped with the remnants of his command.

For his bravery, the nineteen-year-old Tom was breveted a captain of volunteers. More important, the troopers cheered him, and the sound was like a heady wine to him. After months of being an object of their scorn, he found the new experience carried him to heights formerly unknown to him. And he loved the feeling. It set the pattern for his conduct in all future battles, "tweaking the cat's whiskers" for the sheer joy of it. Though he later became something of a boozer, he never found any drink half so intoxicating as risking death in a headlong charge.

The spring rains continued almost daily through March, as the vast Union armies converged on Richmond and Petersburg and the 20 miles separating the last bastions of the Confederacy. The entire area was an ocean of slime. Endless miles of trenches held the Union forces out of Lee's lair.

Sheridan's Cavalry moved slowly toward Petersburg, with the Third Division raiding along the way, destroying crops and anything else of value to the Confederates.

The main target was the Virginia Central Railroad, one of three routes by which Lee might try to escape. The division reached Grant's forces around Petersburg 26 March.

Lee had no chance of victory now; but, if he could escape to North Carolina and merge forces with General Joe Johnston, he might be able to prolong the war long enough to force a negotiated settlement. The two remaining routes he might use for his escape — the Lynchburg and the Richmond and Danville railroads — crossed sixty miles west of the Richmond-Petersburg area. Union control of this junction would end the war.

Sheridan headed west to cut Lee's remaining escape routes, with three divisions of cavalry under Crook, Devin and Custer. The divisions left City Point 27 March, once again in the rain. The Third Division, under Custer, was in charge of the wagons, a low blow to the Custers. Wagons sank hub-deep in mud, barely moved by horses straining against the muck up to their bellies. Tom moved up and down the miles-long line of wagons, shouting encouragement, occasionally dismounting to help empty and shoulder wagons out of the deeper holes. Probably he wouldn't have bothered except that Armstrong did the same thing. Covered with slime, he looked something less than a dashing cavalry officer, but so did those around him.

The rains continued 28 and 29 March, pounding the canvas covers of the wagons like the rapping of drums as the wagon train oozed and slid forward. Whips cracked, men cussed and mules brayed. But most of all, the rain poured, chilling Tom beyond anything he had ever known.

In some semblance of columns, the cavalry snaked onward 30 March, through the dwarf pine forests from which they cut limbs to corduroy their path. But 40,000 hooves soon churned the branches out of sight in the muck. For cavalrymen of Tom's temperament such movement proved torturous.

The division paralleled a flooding creek which the map called Chamberlain's Run, inching along all night. Early on the morning of 31 March, Tom heard the distant rattle of carbines and muskets to the northwest. The other two divisions had made contact with Lee's force trying to keep the escape route open. But the Third Division could only strain and tug along the hundreds of wagons and half-dead mounts and men. And still the rain drenched them, until it became useless to even place tree branches across the dark soup that was supposed to be a road. Time and again a fresh spurt of gunfire raised Tom's hopes of battle.

Relief came at last in the afternoon.

A messenger from General Sheridan ordered Armstrong to leave only one brigade with the wagon train and bring the rest to Dinwiddie Court House. Without the wagons, the division moved considerably faster. It passed through the nondescript village of Dinwiddie Court House and galloped on north. The sound of firing came distinctly now. Cresting a hill, Tom saw lines of Union blue behind breastworks to right and left, stretching beyond sight, firing steadily at mostly unseen foes in the densely wooded area ahead. The discounted troopers broke loose with wild cheers as the Third Division galloped to the rescue in the finest tradition of latter day horse operas.

In the final light of day, the regimental band cut loose with an off-key tune. Then the charge sounded, and once again Tom leaped his mount forward among the leaders. But the horse's forelegs were sunk so deep in the mud the animal flipped rump over forelock, hurling Tom on his backside in the slime. The same fate befell the rest of the line, breaking up the charge before it really began. Rebel fire increased greatly then, reaching for the unhorsed cavalrymen struggling to get back to the protection of their barricades. A battalion already there gave them covering fire. Tom heard the slugs whistle around him, but he made it to safety unharmed, except for his injured pride. What a way for a cavalryman to leave the battlefield.

Darkness closed in before another attack could be organized. Tom prowled all night, too cold and miserable to sleep, and more than a little impatient to get on with the fight.

The first light of day 1 April showed little through heavy mist, but soon the sun melted the soup and Tom could make out the scattered dirt fortifications along the edge of the woods. The Third Division mounted and moved forward at a walk, all the speed possible across the soft ground. Several volleys snarled at them, then the Rebels began pulling back before the steady advance. Many Rebels, too weak from hunger and exhaustion to withdraw and without ammunition for their weapons, surrendered. Mile after slow mile, the Third advanced through the morning against a fighting retreat. At noon they reached the road junction of Five Forks. Not far beyond lay one of Lee's two remaining supply lines and escape routes. At least two miles of log, rail and earthen works protected the wooded area. Cutting it would force Lee to make his run for North Carolina by the other escape route, along the Richmond and Danville Railroad.

The division dismounted to await the arrival of an infantry division. Another cavalry division arrived and dismounted also. Through the afternoon they waited, Tom with diminishing patience. The delay permitted the sun to partially dry out the countryside, promising more effective use of cavalry. The band played most of the time, filling the air with "Yankee Doodle," "Nelly Bly," and other tunes. Most of the men rested.

Finally the infantry division arrived in position far to the right, beyond sight. About 4 p.m., the buglers signaled the men forward at a walk. The tempo soon picked up and Tom found himself across the first line of defense, revolver blazing. The worn out Rebs continued to give way, finally breaking into a rout about dusk.

The Third Division camped for the night on Namozine Creek, not far south of its junction with the Appomattox River. Around the campfire Tom found the men celebrating the end of the war, while various regimental bands filled the air with every tune they knew. Their optimism increased during the night as ragged and starving Rebel deserters approached the camp to surrender.

Lee evacuated Petersburg that night with 80,000 men, fleeing west along various roads in the Appomattox River Valley toward the remaining escape route, the Richmond and Danville Railroad. His troops passed just north of the Third Division campsite.

The second great moment of Tom's life came early 3 April. The Division moved slowly along the Namozine Road until it reached Namozine Creek. Here they found the bridge destroyed, trees felled in the creek to impede fording, and breastworks erected on the west side of the bridge site.

Once again the intoxication of approaching battle rose in Tom. The obvious danger and difficulty of crossing the ford made the tingling sensation all the more delicious. Probably Tom didn't fully understand why he felt that way, nor did he likely give it much thought. For him it was enough that the opportunity was there. He sat his saddle with a growing and nervous impatience while the division moved into position just beyond rifle range of the breastworks.

Armstrong sent one troop upstream perhaps four hundred yards where they dismounted and waded into the creek. Once across, they could outflank the defensive position.

Behind Tom, a cannon opened fire on the breastworks and a gaping hole appeared as a geyser of debris shot upward from the target. It continued booming while another dismounted troop ran toward the site of the bridge, carrying axes to clear the fallen trees from the stream.

The flanking unit cleared the stream and attacked the position from the north, and Tom could wait no longer. He whooped and spurred his mount at the same time. In seconds he reached the stream and galloped on. The tree cutters fell back before his charge. A line of rifle fire searched for him without result, then the Rebels pulled out.

A running fight followed, ever westward along Namozine Road, until it forked near Namozine Church. Here a gray line of cavalry formed for battle.

Again Tom managed to be out front in the first charge against the gray line, which fell back even as it fought. Tom shot his way through the line, the first to break through, and spotted a regimental color bearer. In the Civil War no greater shame befell a unit than to lose its colors under fire. Perhaps that is why more Medals of Honor were awarded for capturing enemy flags than any other act of valor in that war. At any rate, Tom Custer galloped to the colors, whooping his delight. A bullet struck his mount, but it kept moving. With his revolver in his right hand, Tom shot the color bearer out of the saddle. With his left hand he grabbed the colors, as he swept by the riderless mount.

Reining up, Tom whooped again and aimed his revolver at the nearest grayclad, who promptly dropped his own weapon and raised his hands in surrender. Other Rebels followed suit, and in moments Tom had fourteen prisoners, including three officers.

The remaining Rebels surrendered or fled, and the shooting dropped off swiftly. With no other targets, Tom spotted Armstrong nearby and marched his prisoners over to him. But Armstrong had already noticed his reckless brother and smiled his approval. Tom raised the captured colors high, an act greeted by whoops from other troopers. For his valor of that day, Tom Custer was breveted a major and awarded his first Medal of Honor. The division captured 1200 Rebels before the day ended.

The Rebel horse soldiers still free scattered quickly, their delaying action successful but at considerable cost. The Third Division pursued along many trails westward, ever westward toward Lee's rendezvous with the train that would supply him for the trip to North Carolina. Every trail was marked with abandoned guns, burning wagons, crippled or dead horses, and broken down caissons. Without ammunition for their weapons or food for their emaciated bodies, or the slightest hope of eventual victory, the Rebel stragglers, unable to flee any longer, surrendered in numbers greater than the eager Yank cavalrymen cared to capture them. Prisoners slowed them down too much. They wanted to spank the old hound's backside, now that they had him running downhill.

Sheridan's cavalry pressed on westward 4 April. Every dusty trail yielded its stragglers and debris of war. The Third Division reached Jetersville early 5 April. Tom paid scant notice to the hamlet's few shacks. He went with Armstrong to report to Sheridan, where they learned that the main Rebel force was just six miles east at Amelia Court House, another village on the Richmond and Danville Railroad. Lee would have to come through Jetersville to get his sorely needed rations and ammunition now waiting somewhere farther west on the railroad. But that night Lee chose to circle north and bypass Sheridan's forces.

In the pre-dawn light of 6 April, Sheridan sent two cavalry divisions to nip at the rear of Lee's main column and ordered the Third Division to cut cross-country, south of and parallel to the Rebel line of march. The Division moved out in a light mist but with firmer footing than any of the past week. Soon the drizzle gave way to the sun which steamed the countryside.

Twice during the morning, elements of the Division moved close enough to the retreating Rebels to engage briefly. About 11 a.m., the Confederate rearguard — General Ewell's Cavalry and General Anderson's Infantry — halted near Saylor's Creek Valley to permit the miles of wagons to get closer to the head of the column. But the commanders failed to notify the next division up the line of march; consequently, a gap opened in the column ahead of the wagons.

The Third Division had halted to water horses when an aide galloped up with news of the gap. The Third moved out at a gallop to exploit the opportunity, launching the final major battle of the Civil War — a battle that General Sheridan said history failed to give due recognition for the role it played in ending the war. Lee's surrender three days later stole the glory due the Battle of Saylor's Creek.

Tom's first view of Saylor's Creek Valley was from the bluff to the east. The third great moment of his life had arrived. The narrow quarter-mile wide valley ran somewhat north and south, flanked by steep banks on each side. The Creek was actually two branches, Little Saylor's Creek and Big Saylor's Creek. The two branches flowed north a few miles, then joined into a single stream and fed into the Appomattox River.

Coarse swamp grass, mud banks, willow and alder trees

lined the banks of each branch. The area between the creeks was mostly swampy. Four different roads crossed the valley and creeks, all connected by lateral roads.

From his vantage point Tom could see the retreating wagons strung out across the valley. The lead wagons had already crossed Little Saylor's Creek when the Third Division's two light field pieces opened fire. Armstrong dismounted one regiment and formed it into a line which fired at the scattered infantry with the wagons. The rest of the command formed in the scrub trees for another reckless charge. With the field pieces booming and one regiment sniping, the mounted command charged out of the woods with shrill yells. Naturally, Tom Custer galloped in front yelling his glee.

The Rebels held their fire until the first wave neared the wagons, then smoke and flame and lead burst forth to sweep riders from their saddles. Tom emptied his revolver at the gray figures under and around the wagons, while more bluecoats spilled from their saddles. Then the cavalry line broke. With an empty weapon and no support, Tom scooted after his retreating comrades. Even he knew better than to take on the wounded giant alone.

In the woods, Armstrong reformed for another charge while dismounted troopers moved in with carbines. As they neared the wagons, the cavalry charged in again. This time the Rebels could not withstand the onslaught. Defenders still alive surrendered, their scarecrow frames unable to fight anymore.

Burning the hundreds of wagons began then. Soon the smoke from the flames filled the center of the valley. The stench of burning supplies, canvas, wood and leather mingled with the biting odor of death, horse manure and swamps.

The capture of the wagons put the Third Division between Lee's main force and the 8,000 men of Anderson and Ewell, cutting off 10 percent of Lee's total force. The rest of the wagons were destroyed two miles north, where the two branches of the creek converged. This deprived Lee of his critically needed wagon train and part of his artillery — a death blow unless Anderson and Ewell could fight clear.

When the rearguard crossed Little Saylor's Creek, Union infantry opened fire from a hilltop and cavalry charged their flanks. The Rebels struggled on across the swamp bottom and hastily threw up breastworks.

The sound of this fighting reached the Third Division as the captured wagons burned. Tom Custer quickly lost interest in the battle already won. Armstrong caught the same fever, formed the Division and moved out at a gallop. When the Division reached the battle line, the Rebel forces were already weakened by cannon fire and repeated assaults.

But the gray line still had plenty of fight left.

As the Division's band filled the air with stirring music, the troopers charged down the hill, with Tom in the lead once more. Hot lead snarled past him, but left him unhurt. His horse was the first to leap the breastworks through an incredible volley of fire. Tom knee-guided the animal straight toward the color bearer and grabbed the battle flag with his left hand while aiming his revolver with his right. The color bearer refused to turn the flag loose.

Instead, the Rebel shot Tom in the face. The bullet entered his right cheek and came out behind his right ear. Without releasing his hold on the color staff, Tom shot the Rebel and wrenched the staff free. Then he whirled and handed the flag to one of the men who rode up with his brother.

"Armstrong," Tom babbled, "that damned Rebel shot me, but I got his flag."

Then Tom whirled his mount for another charge, but Armstrong stopped him with a shout. Blood spurted from the hole in Tom's cheek and from his ear, and his face was black with burned powder. He weaved in the saddle, close to irrational. Armstrong ordered him to the rear for treatment.

"No," Tom shook his head violently. "Not until the battle is over."

"I order you to the rear," Armstrong snapped, by now greatly concerned for his brother.

Again Tom refused, and tried to gallop off. Armstrong then placed him under arrest and ordered several officers to drag him from the battlefield. As they obeyed, Tom protested vehemently, but the officers took him to a nearby plantation house being used as a field hospital. Here he was treated. For his day's work he received his second Medal of Honor and was breveted a lieutenant colonel. For him, the war was over.

As the day ended, the last of the 8,000 Rebels surrendered, including five generals, one of them General Lee's son, Custis.

Armstrong's rashness finally halted Lee's flight three days later, and the Army of Northern Virginia ceased to exist.

Tom was mustered out 24 November 1865, with two Medals of Honor, having been breveted a lieutenant colonel, though still not old enough to vote. But, for him, additional glory lay ahead on the western plains.

When the army was reorganized in 1866, Armstrong received the permanent rank of lieutenant colonel, second-in-command of the not yet formed Seventh Cavalry. And he secured a lieutenant's commission in the infantry for Tom. Armstrong went to Fort Riley, Kansas, in November 1866, shortly after the nominal commanding officer, Colonel Andrew Smith, started organizing the

Seventh. Then he got Tom transferred to the regiment.

Most easterners regarded the west as a vast wasteland and likened duty there to exile. But for Tom, it meant more opportunity for fighting and glory. The new Seventh Cavalry was a motley collection of war-time officers drastically reduced in rank by the shrunken size of the post-war army, and enlisted men from the backwash of the nation — immigrants, fugitives, escapees from northern slums, and some veterans of both wartime armies. Most of the enlisted men, however, had little or no military training.

Officers spent the winter of 1866-7, trying to whip the troops into a disciplined unit and guarding the construction of the railroad across the endless grassy prairie. Armstrong selected the regimental battle song, "Garry Owen," a tune better suited for barroom carousing but also one that reminded him of galloping horses. Eventually it became a vital morale booster for the regiment. For all practical purposes, Armstrong was the commanding officer, even from the first months.

The Seventh became a part of General Hancock's expedition against hostile Indians in the spring of 1867. A few brushes with hostile bands produced little more than experience for green troops.

Later that year Armstrong was court-martialed and removed from duty for twelve months, for having ordered some fleeing deserters shot, for leaving his command to visit his wife, and for making an unnecessary forced march. In his absence the Seventh accomplished little. It needed its brash commander. And because of this need, especially for a winter campaign against the Cheyenne, General Sheridan recalled him to duty in 1868, before his year of exile was completed. No one welcomed Armstrong's return more than Tom. He had missed the old days of horseplay and battle.

Tom's latest practical joke had occurred when his dog tangled with a skunk, then shared his "charm" with Tom and Captain Hamilton by jumping on them. Such an opportunity could not be wasted. Tom and Hamilton spent the rest of the night going from one officer's tent to another, sharing the "charm" with all the command.

The winter campaign started 12 November 1868, when the Seventh marched south into what is now northwestern Oklahoma and set up a base of operations at Camp Supply. Eleven troops, about 800 men, left Camp Supply at 6 a.m., 23 November, with a foot of snow on the ground and more falling. For Tom, the fourth great moment of his life lay just ahead.

The regimental band rode with them, playing "The Girl I Left Behind Me." Whips cracked over the heads of teams pulling the heavy supply wagons. Visibility was limited to a few hundred yards and the Indian guides and white scouts soon lost their way. But Armstrong used a compass to keep the column moving south. The storm relented the second day, with the snow two feet deep on the prairie. The column moved in a world that appeared to hold no other living things, except for a few buffalo and rabbits.

Tom Custer smiled cockily as the less hardy grumbled about the bitter cold and rugged traveling. A little hardship was small enough price to pay for what lay ahead.

On the fourth day south from Camp Supply, the scouts found the fresh trail of a war party. Each trooper was then issued 100 rounds of ammunition, coffee, hardtack, and forage for his mount. The wagon train was left behind with eighty troopers, and the main command moved on south. About dark 26 November, the command reached sparse timber in the valley of the Washita River.

The thrill of the pursuit gripped Tom now. His only worry was that the hostiles might elude them somehow or that the weakening mounts might not last long enough. They rode on through the night, until the scouts smelled smoke not far ahead on the banks of the Washita River. Cautiously, they moved another half mile before finding the smoldering remains of a single campfire. Tom remained in the saddle while the scouts examined the area. The signs indicated the fire must have been used by Indian boys tending a pony herd. That meant the hostile camp would be within two or three miles father along the river. Once again the command eased forward in a stillness broken only by hooves crunching the crust of the snow.

Tom could just make out the lead Indian scout about midnight, when the sound of barking dogs halted the command. Just ahead grazed a large herd of Indian ponies. The soft tinkle of a bell marked the lead horse of the herd. And somewhere on ahead a baby cried in the darkness. Tom joined the other officers on a hillcrest to stare into the darkness ahead. He could see the dim outline of teepees nestling among trees along the river bank. They studied the terrain for awhile, then Armstrong divided the command into four battalions of something less than 200 troopers each.

Two battalions left immediately, one to circle the area and come up on the far side, the other to take up a position to the right. The third battalion would circle around and come in from the left, but would not leave for about three hours to get into position. The attack would start in four hours. Tom's troop remained in its present position with the main command under Armstrong.

Tom felt weak from the rigors of the trip and tense against the icy cold, and waiting was no easier for him than for his brother. They couldn't even warm themselves by stomping about, because boots breaking through the snow crust crunched loudly in the winter stillness.

Troopers sat around on the snow, some whispering, others silent. Tom wrapped his cavalry cape over his head and sprawled out on the snow for a nap. He woke just before dawn, struggling stiffly to his feet, doubting he would ever thaw out.

All the battalion stirred now, still in silence. Despite the cold, they removed heavy overcoats that would hamper their movements. As light tinged the eastern skyline, they mounted and walked their horses up the hillcrest. Once again the crunching of horses' hooves on the frozen snow sounded loud enough to be heard halfway back to Camp Supply.

As they crossed over the hill and down the far slope, Tom kept listening for a cry or shot from the camp. But the command moved past the pony herd unnoticed, except for the ponies which shied at the strange smell of the intruders.

The battalion reached level ground and continued the advance at a walk, the band bringing up the rear, instruments in hand, ready to play when the charge started. Now Tom could see distinctly the tall white tepees among the trees, smoke curling from their tops.

A single rifle shot from the far side of the village shattered the quiet. Then the bugle sounded the charge and the band blasted forth with "Garry Owen" as the command surged forward with wild yells. Keys on the musical instruments soon froze and silenced the band, but Tom wasn't aware of it. By then all four battalions were pouring fire into the camp as they charged. Half naked warriors tumbled out of the tepees, firing rifles and arrows. Some jumped behind trees. Many didn't make it that far.

Tom guided his mount with knee pressure, using both hands to work his carbine. The village soon emptied and many of the warriors left the trees for the protection of the river bank, standing nearly nude in waist-deep water while firing steadily at the troopers. Powder smoke blackened the snow and clouded the air, hindering the aim of both sides. Tom led his troop from one pocket of resistance to another, exhorting the men to root out the warriors. One bullet knicked Tom's hand but the wound was slight enought to be ignored until later. Flying snowballs kicked up by horses' hooves made him duck several times.

Although outnumbered, the warriors kept up a stiff fire until about 10 a.m. Then those still alive fled down the river, leaving behind only a few snipers to harass the command. A line of troopers was established around the village to keep the snipers at a distance. Mounted warriors began to appear on hills around the village, only a few at first, then up to perhaps a hundred. But little attention was paid to them.

A hospital area for the wounded troopers was set up in the center of the village. So far only two of the command had been killed. But Major Elliott and 18 men were missing. Indian dead totaled 103 warriors, plus some squaws and children. Another 53 squaws and youngsters were brought out of the tepees and formed into a sullen group.

In the tepees the troopers found various items looted from white settlements and isolated ranches — photographs, letters, household items, even dispatches stolen from couriers to General Sheridan.

Armstrong ordered the burning of all the tepees, food and clothing — total destruction of the village. About 875 Indian ponies were rounded up and shot. This left the command short of ammunition, a cause of worry, especially after one of the squaws told them this was the village of the Cheyenne Chief Black Kettle, the first to die in the battle. She also told them that on down the valley, at distances of two to ten miles, lay the villages of all the hostile Arapaho, Cheyenne, Comanche, Kiowa and Apache bands, easily enough warriors to wipe out the Seventh Cavalry if a combined effort was made.

But destruction of the village continued, filling the air with the stench of burning buffalo hides, foodstuffs and other goods. The worry over ammunition eased in the afternoon when a single wagon filled with ammunition from the train rumbled into the camp with warriors at the tailgate. Had the warriors spotted the wagon in time to stop it, the Seventh Cavalry might have been wiped out that day instead of eight years later. The warriors did get the overcoats left behind near the camp, leaving the troopers shivering in the icy air. The command also still had to worry about the wagon train itself, guarded by only 80 troopers and coming closer by the hour. Without that train and its food supply, the troopers could not survive.

Sniper fire increased during the afternoon and small bands of warriors attacked steadily around the line; but when counter-attacked they always fell back, as elusive to contact as smoke from the burning lodges.

The area for two miles around the village was searched, but Major Elliott and his men could not be found. About an hour before dark, the command started down the valley toward the next village. This caused the ring of warriors to hurry on ahead, without knowing the move was a bluff to get them to do just that. After dark the Seventh turned around and moved back through the burned out village. By 10 p.m. they were safe, and the Battle of the Washita was history.

The Seventh Cavalry returned to the area later and recovered the bodies of Major Elliott and his men, making a total of two officers and nineteen men killed there.

Later in the winter the Seventh made an extended expedition across the Oklahoma and Texas plains, tracking down first the Kiowas and later the Cheyennes, taking them back to the Fort Sill Reservation in southwestern Oklahoma Territory. Little combat occurred, but the campaign brought new glory to the regiment, perhaps more deserved than at the Battle on the Washita which was more slaughter than battle. But most of 1869, and 1870, were spent in garrison life at Fort Hays, Kansas, and on routine patrols across the southern plains.

Tom's character degenerated with the boredom of garrison life and patrol duty. Except for courage and audacity, he had few admirable qualities anyway. All his life he had been the darling of the Custer family, pampered, undisciplined. During most of his military years, he had enjoyed the freedom of a doting brother for a commanding officer. Even his brother's wife, Libbie, babied him and made excuses for his shortcomings. And while the Seventh Cavalry had some fine officers and men, it also had its wild and rowdy elements. Few gentle souls could be found among the troopers. Many were the dregs of both east and west, often fugitives from civilian law which seldom reached beyond the corporate limits of frontier towns.

So under this influence, to escape boredom, Tom became a hard drinking, heavy gambling brawler, loudly profane and coarse, who enjoyed smashing saloons. Armstrong strongly opposed this type of conduct and tried to keep a tight rein on Tom in this respect. On one occasion in February 1869, Armstrong had to arrest Tom until he could sober up. But when Armstrong was not around, his little brother was tough for others to handle. Not many cared to cross the brother of the Seventh Cavalry's commander.

In March 1871, the Seventh Cavalry was broken up into smaller detachments, with Armstrong taking two companies to Kentucky. Other detachments, including Tom's troop, were scattered across seven southern states chasing members of the Ku Klux Klan, moonshiners and other criminal elements. Two years later, Tom's troop was reunited again for duty in the Dakota Territory. In June 1873, the command accompanied the Northern Pacific Railroad surveying expedition into the Yellowstone country ceded to the Sioux Indians by treaty. The expedition infuriated the Sioux, bringing on several minor skirmishes.

After the expedition the Seventh marched to Bismarck, North Dakota, a grubby little frontier railroad settlement at the end of the track for the North Pacific Railroad. Bismarck was ideal for the hell-raising Seventh, including Tom Custer, for it contained an abundance of saloons.

Four miles downstream and across the Missouri River, Fort Abraham Lincoln was under construction. This was the final home of the Seventh during the lifetime of the Custer brothers. The fort was typical of those on the frontier at that time: a parade ground surrounded by log barracks and homes for officers. Tom lived in his brother's three-story house, the best residence the family ever enjoyed in the army.

Detachments of the Seventh were scattered to smaller posts in the territory that winter, but most of them were called in the next spring for the fateful Black Hills Expedition in 1874. The trip itself was a violation of the treaty with the Sioux, and its alleged purpose — to locate a site for a fort — was a greater violation. The Black Hills were sacred to the Sioux, who believed their gods dwelled there. It also was their favorite hunting grounds.

Gold was discovered on the expedition, and after word of it reached the depression-stricken east, gold seekers swarmed into the area. When the army failed to keep out the miners, the Sioux began to mutter about a general uprising against the whites. Neither the miners nor the army seemed to worry about the possibility, however.

One incident early in 1875, later grew into a legend about Tom Custer. A young Sioux warrior named Rain-in-the-Face — a member of the tribe at the Standing Rock Agency — boasted of having killed two white men in 1873. One of the Seventh Cavalry scouts overheard him and, from the details, decided the killings had taken place during the Yellowstone expedition. He informed Armstrong, who ordered the Sioux arrested. In response to the order, in the bitter winter of January 1875, Tom and Captain Yates took F Troop 50 miles to the trader's store at the Standing Rock Agency. With six troopers and a Ree scout, Tom went into the store crowded with blanketed Indians bartering for trade goods. He moved about quietly until the Ree scout pointed out Rain-in-the-Face, then he grabbed the warrior by the arms until the troopers could seize him and drag him outside. In the process, they roughed up the Indian and angry Sioux surged forward with murderous intent. Only the leveled carbines of F Troop prevented them from killing Tom. The troopers manacled the Indian, ignoring his threats to cut out Tom's heart and eat it.

Rain-in-the-Face was taken to the guard house at Fort Lincoln, but later escaped. The entire incident likely would have been forgotten except for an incident the following year on the Little Big Horn.

Gold seekers continued to filter into the Black Hills in 1875. The Sioux sizzled, ready to fight. Tom and many others of the Seventh were just as eager. It had been eight long years since the Washita. Parade ground soldiering and monotonous patrols held little appeal for him, though his promotion to captain 2 December 1975, had cheered him some.

Washington tried to buy the Black Hills, but the Sioux wouldn't sell. So, the government ordered all Sioux to return to their reservations by 31 January 1876, or be considered hostile. There wasn't time for most of the Sioux to comply, even had they wanted to, so a summer campaign against them was ordered.

Army strategy for the campaign called for a three-pronged attack. General Crook led one prong north from Fort Fetterman, Wyoming. A second prong came eastward from Fort Ellis, Montana, commanded by Colonel Gibbon. Armstrong led the third prong west from Fort Lincoln. General Terry accompanied the Seventh, in overall command of the two northern columns of Gibbon and Custer.

The most famous of all Indian campaigns and the final big moment of Tom's life began about 6 a.m., 17 May 1876, a morning still foggy from rains of the previous day. Three companies of infantry marched out first, followed by four-horse teams pulling four thousand-round-per-minute Gatling guns. Next came a seemingly endless line of wagons toting the countless tons of ammunition and supplies. It took an hour for this vast array of power to get lined out in the column.

Officers' wives on the verandas and enlisted wives along suds row watched, both proud and fearful. Children marched about beating on tin pans and calling cadence, as if they too were going on the grand adventure. Soldiers left behind to guard the fort stared with envy.

The march began about 7 a.m., when the bugler sounded "to horse" and 12 troops, 600 of the world's finest cavalrymen, mounted in unison. Then "The General" led the main force across the parade ground and out the gate, followed by 60 white and Indian scouts. In all, the column of 1,200 men stretched out for two miles while the regimental band played the regimental fight song, "Garry Owen," "The Girl I Left Behind Me," and other tunes. Surely no Indian rabble could stand against that might.

Tom Custer rode across the parade ground at the head of his C Troop, pulling up at the gate. Some think he carefully planned what he was about to say, and others think it was just the spontaneous enthusiasm characteristic of him at the prospect of battle. For benefit of all who cared to watch and listen, Tom gestured toward the long column.

"A single troop of that," he shouted, "can lick the whole Sioux Nation." Then he and the Seventh Cavalry rode off into legend on the Little Bighorn River.

Five members of the Custer family rode with the Seventh: Armstrong; Tom; another brother, Boston, who came along as a civilian foragemaster; Lieutenant James Calhoun, husband of their sister, Margaret; and a nephew, Autie Reed, a civilian beef herder.

About two weeks west of Fort Lincoln, Tom and Armstrong pulled their last practical joke. They took Boston with them while they rode ahead of the column to locate the best trail through the badlands. When his horse pulled up lame, Boston dismounted.

"There's a pebble in the hoof," he said. While he dug at the pebble, Tom and Armstrong quietly rode around a small hill. On the far side, they dismounted and scurried to the top, clutching their rifles. They peered down, just as Boston finished removing the rock. Boston glanced about for them, hesitated a few seconds, then mounted. Tom and Armstrong fired their rifles over Boston's head, then ducked down. When they raised up again, Boston was 200 yards away and fogging it for the column. Tom and Armstrong fired their rifles again, and Boston kicked his mount into greater effort, certain the entire Sioux Nation was just at his heels. Tom and Armstrong doubled up in convulsions.

The Seventh Cavalry reached the Powder River 7 June, then cut north to the Yellowstone River. Here General

Terry boarded the supply ship **Far West,** leaving Armstrong in command of the overland journey westward, including the cavalry, infantry and Gatling gun detachment. The column followed the Yellowstone past its junction with the Tongue River. One day an Indian "grave" was found in the limbs of a tree. Tom, Boston and Autie Reed pulled it down. It contained the usual items a dead warrior needed on his trip into the hereafter. Young Reed took a bow, six arrows and a pair of moccasins for souvenirs.

About 350 miles from Fort Lincoln, the Rosebud River flows into the Yellowstone. At this point, the Seventh rendezvoused 21 June with the **Far West** and Gibbon's column, both already there. Gibbon set his troops on the north banks with the Seventh on the south side. The final phase of the campaign was planned that day aboard the boat.

Excitement touched everyone now, for trails found by scouts indicated a large encampment of perhaps a thousand Sioux on the Little Bighorn River to the southwest. Gibbon would strike the camp from the north and the Seventh from the east, with each commander timing his marches so his column would arrive there Monday, 26 June. All feared the Indians might escape, so Armstrong was given the prerogative of attacking earlier if he found the hostiles before Gibbon's column arrived.

No word had come from Crook's column. They didn't know that the Cheyenne had defeated the southern force four days earlier and that Crook had retreated. General Terry decided to accompany Gibbon, taking all the infantry and leaving the Seventh alone. He offered the Seventh the Gatling guns, but Armstrong didn't want to be slowed down by the ponderous weapons. Nor did he want part of Gibbon's cavalry. The Seventh could handle anything.

Tom spent his last carefree night aboard the **Far West**, drinking and playing poker. Before leaving near sunup, he filled his canteen with the last whiskey he would ever get. About noon on 22 June, the Seventh started south, riding 12 miles by 4 p.m. and camping there on the banks of the Rosebud.

The fever of the chase began to grow in Tom the next day, as it always did, when the column came upon a fresh Indian trail half a mile wide. The hostile band was a big one. He had no way of knowing this was only one of many fresh Indian trails leading to the Little Bighorn. Like his brother, he worried mostly about the Indians fleeing before their escape could be cut off.

The march continued 24 June, veering more west than south. About noon on 25 June, the column rode down a hillside toward the valley of the Little Bighorn. Some of the scouts claimed they could see a vast pony herd less than twenty miles away, but Armstrong didn't believe them.

Tom could see nothing except a heavy haze the scouts claimed was smoke from the greatest Indian encampment any white man would ever see. A line of timber marked the zigzag course of the Little Bighorn. The Seventh still followed the broad Indian trail, keeping Tom's hopes alive. They might yet catch the hostiles before they could flee.

At this point, Armstrong was supposed to send a message to General Terry, then wait for the joint attack. But he told his officers he didn't believe the Indians were there. More likely, he just didn't want to share the glory.

When the Seventh reached the valley floor, Armstrong divided the command into three battalions. Captain Benteen took three companies totaling 128 men and rode to the left. He would circle to the south. Major Reno with three troops totaling 112 men would hit the campsite in the center. Armstrong kept five troops — 225 men — including Tom's C Troop, and would hit the north flank. One troop would remain with the pack train. The scouts were divided among the three battalions.

Benteen soon rode out of sight to the south. The other two battalions rode along each side of a stream that fed the Little Bighorn, each following an Indian trail. Dust from thousands of hooves choked them, and the heat wilted them, but Tom paid such discomforts little heed. He had room only for excitement now. It had been eight long years since the Washita.

The miles fell behind the column without sight of hostiles, but the broad fresh trail remained. They rode up to a single tepee and found a dead Sioux inside. The Ree scouts set it on fire. The first Indians were sighted then, about 2:15 p.m., 40 or so warriors who quickly fled westward toward the Little Bighorn. There could be no waiting for Gibbon now. The hostiles would vanish long before he could arrive the next day. Armstrong ordered Reno to attack straight ahead, along the Indian trail, while he led his five troops northwestward along a parallel course, in the hills on the north side of the river.

Reno crossed the river and followed it northwestward also, until Sioux suddenly swarmed at the battalion about 3 p.m. Reno could see enough of the village ahead to know it was massive, far beyond what they had expected. Instead of fleeing, the Sioux and Cheyenne pressed the attack. Reno formed a skirmish line 200 yards west of the river. On the north side of the river, the main battalion could see the dust from Reno's skirmish. Jubilation swept the command then. The hostiles wouldn't escape now.

Armstrong ordered a sergeant to find Captain McDougall and tell him to bring the pack train straight across country — come quick — big Indian village — tell

Benteen to come quick.

The battalion moved on northwestward, still parallel to the river and somewhat away from Reno's position. It reached a bluff overlooking a camp five miles long and ten miles wide. As the scouts had warned, the camp was the biggest one ever encountered by white men — three tribes of the Sioux Nation plus the Northern Cheyenne, totaling perhaps 13,000 Indians of which maybe 5,000 were warriors. No one could determine exact numbers at the time, though the size of the camp was warning enough. But the battalion was still eager for a fight, none more so than Custer.

Some historians think it was Armstrong's intention to attack the village and place the battalion at the rear of the warriors tearing apart Reno's command. Others believe that as the battalion moved down toward the river to cross it, a handful of warriors hidden behind a rise opened fire causing Armstrong to take up a defensive position. This latter seems unlikely. For 15 years Armstrong had followed only one battle tactic — attack first, without regard to the size of the enemy, and if unable to overcome him, fight clear.

For whatever reason, the battalion set up in a defensive position five miles upstream from a hill to which Reno had by now retreated with what was left of his command. Benteen's battalion was there also, having encountered no Indians on the southern swing. Neither of the two groups knew the location or predicament of the other. But both were surrounded and under heavy attack by more Indians than they had earlier thought possible.

Dust churned up by thousands of horses and smoke from thousands of firearms clouded the valley and hills. Stinging heat drenched troopers with sweat that turned the dust into damp filth. It was difficult to recognize even a close friend only a few feet away.

As late as 5 p.m., the main battalion was still in a sound defensive position, without heavy casualties. But the rough terrain around the position provided the best possible cover for the hostile snipers. Gradually the circle drew tighter around the command, with most of the Indians on foot. On the down-slope side where the least natural cover existed, horses were led out in a semi-circle and shot, their bodies then forming a barrier to protect the most exposed flank of the Seventh. Behind this protection, the officers of the battalion held a war conference — no panic — but situation serious — they needed the battalions of Reno and Benteen.

Three troops were assembled, and on command they fired two volleys. It mattered little, for Reno and Benteen were pinned down also, and could have been overrun at any time.

The sound of battle at Custer's position soon ceased forever.

The attack on Reno's hill ended at dark. The troopers spent the night digging holes and forming breastworks, knowing they could not withstand an all-out assault. Terror gripped many, determination others. In the valley below, the Indians whooped it up all night. Some historians claim the Indians staged an all-night victory dance, and others claim it was mourning for their dead. The latter seems most likely, considering the price the Indians had already paid for a victory not yet complete.

With daylight 26 June, the attack on Reno's hill resumed but the expected massive assault did not come. Late in the day sniper fire ceased and the hostiles withdrew. Then the Indian camp began pulling out of the valley in a loose line that seemed endless. Why the Indians did not finish the job will never be known, although many speculations from whites and "true accounts" from Indians have been published.

General Terry arrived with Gibbon's column on the morning of 27 June. It reached Custer's position first, finding the entire command of 225 wiped out, most of them stripped and mutilated. All but three of the officers — including the three Custers — were together behind the arc of horses.

Tom Custer was slashed and crushed almost beyond recognition. All his hair had been scalped and his skull crushed. A dozen arrows protruded from his body. The stomach was ripped open and the heart cut out. The latter fact stirred memories of the previous year when Rain-in-the-Face swore he would someday cut out Tom's heart and eat it. A reporter claimed he asked Rain-in-the-Face if he had eaten Tom's heart and that the Indian had replied, "Some of it."

It is possible that the Indians made the boast because many plains Indians enjoyed shocking naive white men. But no historian of stature believes Rain-in-the-Face actually did eat Tom's heart; cannibalism was as abhorrent to the plains Indians as it was to the whites.

The three Custer brothers were buried side by side on the hill where the two became legends. Armstrong later was removed to the cemetery at West Point. In death, Tom and Armstrong achieved the glory they pursued all their adult lives. For all their many weaknesses, they had at least one redeeming quality — unexcelled raw courage.

National Archives

FIRST DOUBLE WINNER Capt. Thomas Ward Custer.

FIRST DOUBLE WINNER Capt. Thomas Ward Custer (arrow, second from right) is shown here with a party from Fort Abraham Lincoln, Dakota Terrotory, at Little Heart River, in 1875. Less than a year later Tom and seven others shown here were killed in action (KIA) at the Battle of the Little Big Horn, Montana. Others shown are (left to right) Lt. James Calhoun (Tom's brother-in-law, KIA), Mr. Sweet, Capt. S. Baker, Boston Custer (Tom's brother, KIA), W. S. Edgerly, Miss Watson, Capt. Miles Keogh (KIA), Mrs. James Calhoun (Tom's sister), Mrs. George Armstrong Custer (Tom's sister-in-law), General George Armstrong Custer (Tom's brother, KIA), Dr. H.S. Paulding, Mrs. A. E. Smith, Dr. G. E. Lord (KIA), Capt. T. B. Weir, Lt. W. W. Cooke (KIA), Lt. R. E. Thompson, Miss Wadworth and Miss Wadworth, Tom Custer (KIA), and Lt. A. E. Smith (KIA).

CHAPTER TWO

John Cooper
(1832-91)

The Navy's first double winner of the Medal of Honor was a jaunty little Irishman, five feet, four inches tall, with sandy hair and gray eyes. Born John L. Mather, probably 28 July 1828 (his Navy record lists 1832), he came to the United States as a child. When he enlisted in the Navy at the age of 17, 1 August 1845, he changed his last name to Cooper for some unknown reason. And Cooper he remained.

Cooper served his first four years aboard the frigate **USS Congress**, recommissioned 15 September 1845, in Norfolk. She sailed for the Pacific in October 1845, and joined the Pacific Squadron in Monterey Bay. The squadron patrolled the coast of California during the war with Mexico. Cooper fought with the Naval landing forces near San Diego and Los Angeles, and at Guaymas (October 1847) and Mazatlan (November 1847), Mexico. He was discharged 5 February 1849, in Norfolk, Virginia.

For the next 15 years, Cooper sailed out of New York as a merchant ship mariner. He married Mary O'Keefe there 23 January 1856, and fathered five children. He again enlisted in the U.S. Navy 16 April 1864, in New York, as a coxswain, and earned his first Medal of Honor only four months later.

Fog shrouded Mobile Bay, Alabama, early the morning of 5 August 1864, hiding it from the U.S. Naval Squadron at anchor outside the bay. On watch at his bow gun on the **USS Brooklyn**, Cooper stared into the fog. Pilings closed off most of the harbor entrance and could rip the wooden bottom out of the **Brooklyn**, torpedoes (mines) across most of the narrow channel could blast her apart, the guns of high-up Fort Morgan could rain the wrath of Satan down on the squadron, and finally — in the bay itself, if they made it that far — the **Tennessee**, the south's best ironclad, waited.

The **Brooklyn** had 20 nine-inch Dahlgren guns, plus two 100-pound and two 60-pound Parrot rifles — making her a regular floating gun platform officially listed as a twin-screw type steam sloop. And with her 11-knot speed, the **Brooklyn** could outmaneuver the **Tennessee** if she could just get into the bay without critical battle damage. The old girl would give a good account of herself.

Eighty-seven bluejackets in the squadron — twenty-two of them aboard the **Brooklyn** — would earn Medals of Honor that day. Of the group, only Cooper would later earn a second award and become the Navy's first double winner.

The smell of nearby land lay heavy in the air. Shivering against the bite of the cold dampness against his naked chest, Cooper listened to the clanking of heavy anchor chains draped over the sides of the hull as improvised armor. Not all of the 233-foot length was covered — only the most vital portions. Sandbags protected the exposed decks and bulkheads. Nets hung from the masts to catch flying splinters that would come from exploding shells. Rigged to the bow was a hoist for picking up mine-type torpedoes or carrying a torpedo for ramming into the **Tennessee**, if the chance occurred.

The fog thinned some about 4:30 a.m., as a breeze picked up a little. Cooper could see other ships now, rocking gently in the fairly calm sea. Each of seven small wooden ships came along the port side of a larger wooden ship, the side that would be away from the guns of Fort Morgan as they entered the bay. The **Brooklyn** paired off with the smaller **Octotora**. Bluejackets then passed over heavy cables and the ships were snubbed together. This was protection for both. If either ship in a pair was hit in the hull, its partner might be able to keep it afloat long enough to make emergency repairs.

By 5:30 a.m., the breeze blew strong enough to dissipate the rest of the fog and the squadron formed a line. The boatswain piped battle stations, and Cooper returned to his bow gun as the ships lined up for the run past Fort Morgan. By then the sun warmed him. The day, now bright and clear, would be perfect for closing the South's one remaining major seaport on the Gulf.

Four ironclads led by the **Tecumseh** formed a line to the starboard side of the wooden vessels in order to take the brunt of the fire from Fort Morgan. Both lines of ships bore down on the narrow channel on the east side of the harbor mouth.

Cooper ordered his guncrew to remove their boots to lessen the chance of accidentally igniting grains of powder that would inevitably sift from bags to the deck during the loading of the weapon. Then he ordered the tampion (plug) removed from the muzzle. Powder monkeys trotted up from the magazine below decks with cloth bags of powder for the four bow guns. Loaders brought shells from the shell whips behind the gun and these, too, went down the muzzle. Cooper stood by the firing lanyard, ready to fire on command.

Fort Morgan was perched high above the bay on the right, but not yet in gun range. That meant the ship was getting close to the two rows of torpedoes — about 200 in all — anchored seven feet under the surface and stretching from the pilings across all but the last 300 feet of the channel, the 300 feet nearest the guns of Fort Morgan. That wasn't much room for lines of ships, even without the fort to guard it. The torpedoes were set to explode on contact with the vessels.

The leading monitor **Tecumseh**, almost even with the **Brooklyn**, opened the battle with a salvo about 7 a.m., and shells exploded over the fort. Cooper tensed for return fire, but for several moments only silence came from the fort. Then he saw a large puff of smoke billow from the fort, and a long slash of flame shot out of the smoke, followed by a muffled boom. An explosion off the starboard bow of the **Brooklyn** sent a spout of water mushrooming upward.

Cooper yanked on the firing lanyard almost simultaneously with other gunners. Smoke and flame belched forth from the bow, obscuring vision. The **Brooklyn** trembled under Cooper's bare feet, then concussion crushed in and sucked out of his midriff and jiggled his eyeballs.

"Reload," he shouted. A crewman with a long-handled plunger swabbed sparks out of the barrel. Loaders packed in double charges again and added the shot. Cooper adjusted the elevation and side-to-side controls, sighting on the fort guns, then pulled the firing lanyard. He soon lost count of the rounds fired.

A blast far greater than the roar of cannons rocked the air, and Cooper saw a gigantic water spout shoot up alongside the bow of the monitor **Tecumseh**. The ironclad had hit a torpedo and was sinking. The squadron was directly under the guns of Fort Morgan now. The bow lookout on the **Brooklyn** shouted that he could see torpedo buoys dead ahead. When the word reached the bridge, engines were reversed and the **Brooklyn** shuddered to a halt. Shells from the fort guns found the range of the **Brooklyn**, and Cooper could hear the explosions and feel the vibrations of the deck as the ship took hit after hit. But he was too busy to look around.

The **Hartford** swerved around the port side from its position second in line, passing the **Brooklyn**. Her bow slashed through the line of torpedoes. Cooper could hear the torpedoes bumping and scraping against the **Hartford's** hull — but none exploded.

Powder smoke blinded Cooper now, and he rubbed at his burning eyes. Despite the continuous roar of guns and exploding shells, Cooper could hear the patter of barefooted powder monkeys running back and forth from the powder magazine.

An explosion between the two shell whips behind Cooper killed or wounded all crewmen there. The screams of the wounded cut the air but Cooper remained at his station. Some of his crew cast fearful glances at the carnage behind them, but he snarled at them and they resumed their loading.

Splinters from another blast needled Cooper's backside, causing him to pull the firing lanyard almost before the loaders were clear of the muzzle.

Crewmen cleared away the debris of the demolished shell whips behind him and rigged a new one; but before it was put into operation another shot from the fort hit the same spot, again clearing out every man there. Once again Cooper exerted his will over the more timid of his crew.

Finally the **Brooklyn** drew out of range of the fort guns only to find the Rebel ironclad **Tennessee** and three small gunboats bearing down on the squadron. The **Tennessee** opened fire on the **Hartford**, now leading, heavily damaging the wooden foe. Shells from the **Hartford** glanced or bounced off the armor plating of the **Tennessee**. The **Brooklyn's** turn came next. She took the same kind of pounding while her shells failed to penetrate the iron hull, even at point blank range. There was no missing a target that size and that close, and no damaging her either.

The **Tennessee** attacked all the way down the line, finally anchoring directly under the guns of Fort Morgan. The Union squadron moved up the bay four miles and anchored also, minus one monitor and four wooden ships now on the bottom of the bay.

Aboard the **Brooklyn** the dead and wounded were removed, but little attempt was made at patching up massive battle damage. Instead, the boatswain piped breakfast. Mess cooks spread cloths on the grimy and bloody deck, then set out pans, spoons and cups. Large pots of pork, potatoes, molasses and coffee were put in the center of each cloth. Cooper led his guncrew to the nearest spread, and sat cross-legged on the deck. He spooned his tin plate full and wolfed down the food, wondering if he would have time to finish before the **Tennessee** attacked again. He did, barely.

Half an hour after anchoring, the **Brooklyn** sounded battle stations and Cooper returned to his gun as the anchor chain was hauled in. Four miles away the **Tennessee** had rammed the **Ironclad**, ripping away her own iron bow without denting the Union ship. The flagship **Hartford** was next in line, ramming the **Tennessee** at an angle and glancing off without damaging the iron hulk. Pulling away, she fired a broadside so close its powder burned the **Tennessee** without damaging her.

The Union monitors attacked then, one ramming at full speed with little result except to crush her own bow. But a nine-inch shell jammed one of the shutters that opened each time the gun behind it was ready to fire. The shutter now couldn't be opened, eliminating part of the

Tennessee's firepower. Another sloop rammed and fired a broadside without effect, except to jam another gunport shutter. The squadron surrounded the **Tennessee** now, raking her with scorching but apparently ineffective fire. Finally the monitor **Chickasaw** found one weak spot on the Rebel craft. Coming in astern, she shot away the exposed rudder chain and left the **Tennessee** unable to maneuver but still deadly, and with a hull and casemate invulnerable to gunfire.

Cooper found the final weak spot. Frustrated in his attempts to dent the hull, he elevated his gun and aimed at the smokestack. His shell blasted away the pipe, causing the inside of the ship to fill with smoke from the boilers. The **Tennessee** soon surrendered.

The battle for Mobile Bay ended about 10 a.m., after three hours. The victory closed the last major Gulf port of the Confederacy. The Union squadron and ground troops next forced the surrender of the forts. For his courage under fire, particularly for remaining at his gun station and keeping her crew there in an exposed position, Cooper received his first Medal of Honor. Most of the 22 awards to **Brooklyn** crewmen were for similar heroism.

The **Brooklyn** suffered 11 dead and 43 wounded. She was struck 60 times, including 25 shots through the hull. Shells sieved one berthing space, ruined the mainmast, knocked out two guns and smashed all but two lifeboats.

The ship went to the Boston Naval Station for repairs, then joined the North Atlantic blockading squadron until the attack 24-25 December on Fort Fisher, North Carolina, the South's final link with the outside world. The attack failed and was repeated 13 January 1865.

Cooper was back on his bow gun when the **Brooklyn** led the first battle line that moved in on the fort about 5 a.m. The ship ran parallel to the beach, about 600 yards out, shelling the woods north of the fort, as General Terry's ground forces landed from boats nearby. For six hours Cooper fired at the Rebel positions, while 6,000 soldiers went ashore. The **Brooklyn** dropped out of the line then and came back at 4 p.m. and fired until dark.

The following afternoon the **Brooklyn** shelled the fort for three hours. Other ships took turns on the line, firing all day and night, smashing at the fort. Another day of bombardment followed until the fort surrendered about 9:30 p.m., 15 January 1865.

In March the **Brooklyn** returned to Mobile Bay to help ground forces capture the city. She fired artillery support to the troops. When Lee surrendered, she remained on station in the bay.

Cooper became a quartermaster on the staff of Rear Admiral H. K. Thatcher and temporarily went aboard the flagship, the **USS Stockdale**. On the morning of 26 April 1865, he heard a tremendous explosion over in the city of Mobile. A column of smoke and flames shot up from a large warehouse about three-quarters of a mile from where the ship lay at anchor. Ammunition captured from the Confederates had been stored in the building and now began exploding in a chain reaction from the swiftly spreading flames. Shell fragments fell on the deck of the ship, causing some of the bluejackets to take cover.

Fleet Admiral Simpson called for volunteers to go ashore and help fight the blaze. Cooper was one of 50 to step forward.

Two longboats carried the volunteers ashore, then they double-timed to the stricken area. Already many civilians and soldiers lay dead or wounded in the streets, mostly from flying shell fragments.

The sailors joined the fire fighting but were continuously pushed back by the fury of the flames and by exploding shells. Shrapnel killed two of the sailors and struck down a third about 50 yards from Cooper. Fresh blasts sent shrapnel snarling in all directions, and burning buildings on both sides of the unconscious bluejacket seemed ready to collapse.

Unmindful of both dangers, Cooper dodged through flaming debris to reach his wounded shipmate. He bent over the still form, finding the man still alive. Somehow the little Irishman hoisted the larger man on his shoulders and carried him to safety. For this act he received his second Medal of Honor.

Cooper received an honorable discharge 11 October 1866, from the **USS Vermont**. He returned to New York and resumed his career as a merchant mariner for the next eleven years, until disabled by an injury. He died of a heart ailment 14 years later, 22 August 1891, in Sailor's Snug Harbor Hospital, Staten Island, New York. He is buried in Cypress Hills National Cemetery.

U. S. Navy Photograph

SECOND DOUBLE WINNER *John Cooper earned both of his Medals of Honor while serving aboard this ship, the USS BROOKLYN, receiving the first medal in 1864 and the second in 1865.*

CHAPTER THREE

Patrick Mullen
(1838-?)

Another Irishman, 24-year-old Patrick Mullen, began a three-year enlistment as a landsman in the U.S. Navy 13 August 1862, at Baltimore, Maryland. With light skin and dark hair and eyes, he stood only five feet, nine inches but managed to earn promotion to boatswain's mate so he must have been handy with his fists.

During the final year of the Civil War, Mullen served aboard the screw steamship **USS Don** on countless expeditions up Virginia creeks and rivers. Smuggling was the South's only remaining means of securing outside help. As flagship for the Potomac River Flotilla, the **Don** waged daily war against boats and waterway bases of smugglers and the guerrilla forces of Major Mosby. On one of these expeditions Mullen won the first of his two Medals of Honor. His second award came only five days after Cooper became the Navy's first double winner.

The **Don** took command of the Potomac River Flotilla in May 1864. The 180-foot, 400-ton ship was one of the first twin-propeller steamers ever built. Though adequately armed, her main advantage was speed and shallow draft, both important in inland waterways operations.

The logbook of the **Don** records with regularity the destruction of boats and bases. The Flotilla destroyed 17 boats 27 September 1864, on the Virginia shore opposite Charles County, Maryland. Then a large Rebel craft was discovered up the Rappahannock River 16 October. The **Don** sent a boarding party in three boats to capture her. Mullen manned the bow howitzer of the lead launch. As the boats approached the shore, guerrillas ashore opened fire with muskets and some rifles. Answering cannon fire from the **Don** whistled over Mullen's head and raked the shoreline, driving away the snipers. The boarding party then set fire to the Rebel ship.

In the Great Wicomico River of Virginia on 26 October, the **Don** steamed within view of a scattering of houses used as shelter by Rebel forces. Light cannon fire searched for the **Don**, but a few broadsides soon silenced the artillery. Mullen accompanied the landing party that drove the Rebels away and burned the three houses.

The **Don** went up Passpatansy Creek, Virginia, 5 March 1865, looking for a large boat that military intelligence had learned would soon be used for a raid into Maryland. When they found the boat, Mullen went ashore with the 75-man attacking force and engaged Mosby's guerrillas for more than an hour, then burned the boat. At daylight 6 March, the **Don** steamed in to within 200 yards of a Rebel field piece on Jones Bluff overlooking the Rappahannock River and knocked out the weapon with a single broadside. The Flotilla then returned to its base for resupply.

St. Inigoes Creek (Maryland) Naval Base hardly deserved so pretentious a name. A supply ship and floating wharf provided its chief reason for existence, but it was home for the **Don** for the final year of the war.

The Flotilla left St. Inigoes about 7 p.m., 15 March 1865, on the most important expedition of Mullen's naval service. The steamers **Stepping Stone, Heliotrope,** and **Resolute** strung out behind the **Don** down the Potomac River.

Mullen knew little about the expedition, except that it was to knock out another Rebel base somewhere. The call to battle stations sent him to his gun station on the bow about daylight 16 March, when the **Don** turned from the Potomac into Mattox Creek, Virginia. The throb of the ship's 250-horsepower engines softened as the ship slowed to minimize the hazards of the shallow water. Coal smoke from the ship's stack mingled with light mist but quickly fell back as the **Don** moved on steadily.

Mullen kept a close watch on the west bank, ready to fire at any target of opportunity. Well inland from the Potomac, the creek curved westward and widened where it forked into two branches. A cluster of buildings that probably passed for a hamlet sprawled on the south side near the fork. The mist had cleared now, but thick tree branches shaded the area. Still Mullen saw several figures flee the houses and dart into the woods.

Suddenly the **Don** grounded on a sandbar, and Mullen grabbed his howitzer to keep from falling to the deck. The other ships also grounded, but there was no time to get them off the bars.

Mullen went ashore with the landing party of 40 men and 1 ensign. They searched each house without finding any Rebels. Then Mullen led the three Negro landsmen into a barn where they found six bales of tobacco and a large quantity of ammunition. This they carried back to the landing boats.

The level of the creek rose in the afternoon, floating all the ships except the **Heliotrope** off the sandbar by the time the landing party embarked. The **Heliotrope** floated free during the night.

The next morning the deck crew lowered a howitzer launch into the water. Mullen manned the small howitzer mounted on the bow. Ensign Summers, commanding the launch, sat in the stern and manned the rudder. Other crewmen, all Negro landsmen, manned the oars. The launch moved slowly and silently up the right fork of the creek, while 70 men marched along the banks. From some underbrush, several snipers opened fire on the land force. Ensign Summers brought the launch around and Mullen swiveled his howitzer, but the firing ceased before he could sight on the hidden foe.

Farther down the creek, Mullen spotted four boats along the bank and waved the land force to the spot. While they destroyed the boats, Summers turned the launch around and returned to the junction of the two prongs. On the bridge of the **Don** a signalman ordered the launch up the left prong — without waiting for the land force. The launch crew didn't care much for going up the creek alone, but they resumed rowing on orders.

Mullen grinned a little at their discomfort. Landsmen just didn't appreciate what a bluejacket considered "the finer things in life."

This fork of the creek appeared to be deeper — perhaps deep enough for larger craft. This, and the danger of snipers from either shore, sharpened the senses of Mullen. One small-caliber howitzer wouldn't count for much against the weapons of some of the vessels capable of going up this fork.

For a time only the squeaking of oarlocks and the gentle swish of water broke the stillness. Then the launch rounded a bend to a widened, lake-like area. Three schooners lay just ahead, along piers on the left bank.

"Get set," Ensign Summers called softly.

Mullen needed no such advice. He sighted the howitzer on the nearest schooner but could see no one aboard. All three schooners seemed deserted.

When the launch drew to within 50 yards of the nearest schooner, a single musket cracked from the underbrush on the left bank, followed immediately by a chain of firing all along the creek. Mullen swiveled the howitzer as bullets buzzed all around him. Several slugs ripped through the gunwales of the launch. Then Mullen fired the howitzer. The blast deafened him and threw him back against the starboard gunwale, but even as he fell back Mullen saw flame spurt up from the underbrush, hurling a body high into the air. Some 400 muskets sniped at the launch then. The landsmen hunched down for the dubious protection afforded by the gunwales.

"Keep rowing," Mullen shouted. And the oars dipped back and forth, not completely in unison but mighty fast. Mullen then ignored the snipers while he dug three firebombs out of the ready box. Fortunately, they had apparently caught the Rebels unprepared; the schooners were unmanned. One well-placed cannon shot would have ended the expedition quickly. When the launch reached the first schooner, Mullen lit the fuse on a firebomb and stood up in the boat. Somehow all 400 snipers missed him as he arched the bomb on the deck of the schooner and dropped back behind the gunwale. The oarsmen worked fast then to get the schooner between the launch and the snipers. When the firebomb exploded, flames spurted across the deck of the schooner. Mullen hurled a second firebomb aboard the next schooner and a third one on the last craft. All three soon blazed furiously.

Ensign Summers reversed course and the launch started back downstream, putting them under sniper fire again. But this time Mullen kept up a steady return fire with the howitzer. The recoil seemed like it would rip the bow off the launch. The constant snarl of bullets from the shore forced him to lie on his back to load the howitzer, and raise up only to sight and fire. Frequently the bullets came right on through the gunwales. One after another of the oars was smashed by bullets.

Ensign Summers, in the stern, fired a musket at the

shore until a bullet smashed the barrel from the stock.

Mullen used the flash and smoke of muskets for targets, hitting them with consistent accuracy. One official report said he killed "more than a score," and his citation said he killed and wounded "many." His prowess with the howitzer, and his courage in using it while the target of 400 snipers, shattered the Rebel force and forced the survivors to flee. For this service he received his first Medal of Honor.

Less than half the oarsmen had anything left to row with for the return down the creek. Perhaps it was just as well, for the rest of the crewmen barely kept the launch afloat by bailing furiously the water sloshing in through the numerous bullet holes in the gunwales. One slightly wounded landsman was the only Union casualty.

By late afternoon the launch reached the **Don**. Mullen went ashore and helped set up a fortified position. The land force cut down trees and ripped apart 200 feet of fencing to build a barricade. Then they burned a nearby shed to leave a clear field of fire. A heavy guard remained awake all night.

About daylight the grayclads attacked, coming out of the woods in two columns; but they fired only a few rounds and fled before the Yanks could put up an effective return fire. That ended the battle of Mattox Creek.

The Flotilla returned to river patrol duty, occasionally capturing a small boat of contraband and two or three smugglers. In mid-April, the **Don** captured a schooner near the Virginia shore of the Potomac. It was also active in the search for the assassin of President Lincoln, searching all vessels encountered.

Six weeks after earning his first Medal of Honor, Mullen distinguished himself again. The Flotilla was on patrol the night of 1 May 1865, probably in Chesapeake Bay, when a storm hit. The 180-foot **Don** took the pounding well, but some of the smaller craft bobbed about like shoe boxes, half the time with their stern sections under water.

Among the assorted smaller craft of the Flotilla was one listed only as Picket Launch No. 6, sailing off the starboard quarter of the **Don**. Mullen, on boatswain's watch, could see the launch was in trouble from the amount of water she was taking. At one point she plunged from the top of a giant swell into the depths of a trough and swamped.

The **Don** came about to pick up survivors. Mullen organized a group of seamen on the quarterdeck to throw lines to the crewmen. The **Don** couldn't get too close to the swamped launch without grave risk of collision, so the crewmen had to swim out a ways to catch the lines. The best swimmers were pulled aboard first, half drowned. It didn't take long to swallow and inhale a lot of water in seas that rough.

One of the survivors, a young officer, barely able to swim, fell behind the others. The gap between him and the nearest crewman gradually widened. At times swells hid him completely. Finally, he dropped into a trough and didn't come up when the water swelled up the next time.

Mullen, already barefoot for better traction on a wet deck, jumped to the gunwale and leaped into the sea. His normally strong swimming strokes seemed feeble against the might of the waves. In the minutes it took to reach the spot where the officer had gone under, Mullen never once saw him. But, at just the right moment, a hand broke the surface and Mullen grabbed it. He pulled the officer over on his back and lifted his face out of the water, cupped his chin in his left hand and began swimming toward the **Don**, not at all certain the young man was still alive.

Fighting the swells with one hand seemed almost useless at times, especially when they dropped into a trough, but riding the tops of the swells made some progress possible. He lost track of time and only dimly saw the **Don** when a line finally reached him. He used it to pull himself and the officer closer to the ship, then secured it around the officer's chest. The crew pulled them aboard.

The young officer did revive, and Mullen received his second Medal of Honor.

Two months later, the Potomac Flotilla was disbanded. Mullen was honorably discharged 17 July 1865, at Baltimore. His service was, and remains, an almost unknown chapter in the backwash of the Civil War.

CHAPTER FOUR

Frank Baldwin
(1842-1923)

Frank Dwight Baldwin, the U.S. Army's second double winner of the Medal of Honor and its only hero ever recommended for a third award, was as modest as Tom Custer was arrogant. He spent a lifetime avoiding fame while still pursuing hazardous service in the Civil War, Indian campaigns and in the Philippines. A deadly foe, without fear, he was as resourceful and dependable an officer as the American military system is ever likely to produce. Dark, stockily built but not tall, quiet, dedicated, and cool-under-fire, he was an unpretentious warrior of the old army.

Born 26 June 1842, in Manchester, Michigan, Baldwin was educated in the Constantine, Michigan public schools and at Hillsdale (Michigan) College. He received a commission as second lieutenant in the Michigan Volunteers (Horse Guard) 19 September 1861, at the age of 19. His company was mustered out two months later. The following 5 September, he was commissioned a first lieutenant in the 19th Michigan Volunteers.

Baldwin's first battle came 25 March 1863, when his mounted infantry pursued Confederate forces in Tennessee. The Yanks overtook the Rebs six miles from the town of Brentwood. In a brief skirmish, the Blues overpowered the smaller Confederate force, but Rebel reinforcements routed the initial victors, capturing Baldwin among 759 prisoners. He was taken to the infamous Andersonville prisoner-of-war camp, but the South soon exchanged him for a Rebel officer. He rejoined his regiment at Fort Rosecrans, near Murfreesboro, Tennessee.

Baldwin was in command of Company D 13 September 1863, when he volunteered the company to man a stockade four miles south of the fort. The stockade overlooked a railroad bridge across Stone River. His mission was to prevent destruction of the bridge. That afternoon he led 50 enlisted men out of Fort Rosecrans on a march down the Louisville, Nashville and Chattanooga Railroad tracks on the east bank of the river.

Baldwin found the stockade to be a fairly strong defensive position. Except for the river bed, the surrounding country stretched out flat and almost treeless, offering no cover for attacking forces. Six-inch logs stuck two feet into the ground and eight feet above ground formed a 25-foot square stockade. Through chest-high loopholes, the troops could pick off anyone on or near the 200-foot-high wooden trestle spanning the river, but the lightest of artillery could wreck the log walls with a round or two.

To strengthen the position, Baldwin ordered the men to shovel dirt embankments against both sides of the walls. By the time they finished this chore, it was getting dark so he ordered a large Sibley tent set up inside the walls. It slept 17 men. The rest of the men set up their tents outside the stockade.

For three weeks the company loafed around the stockade, but on 4 October several mounted Rebel parties passed within a mile or two of the post. Each paused long enough to study the fortification. Baldwin sent a runner to Fort Rosecrans, where 9,000 Union soldiers were garrisoned; but despite his request, he received no reinforcements. Apparently it was thought his company could withstand any assault long enough for help to arrive.

Baldwin's thoughts didn't dwell upon his precarious position that night; his only concern was preparing for assault. He was up early 5 October, studying the terrain to the east. Light rain limited visibility, so he alerted the entire command to be ready. The rain ceased, and about 8 a.m. Baldwin spotted several troops of Confederate cavalry approaching slowly from the east. The force halted well out, and a dozen or so horsemen came on, showing a white flag of truce.

"Don't fire without orders," Baldwin cautioned. With one of his sergeants, he walked slowly toward the mounted men who stopped about a hundred yards from the stockade.

"What is your mission?" Baldwin asked with characteristic politeness.

Equally polite, the leader identified himself as the adjutant for General Wheeler, commanding 10,000 cavalry and supporting artillery.

"In the name of General Wheeler, I demand your immediate and unconditional surrender," the officer said.

"Sorry," Baldwin shook his head. He told the officer that his orders were to guard the bridge against destruction. He had already notified the commanding general at Fort Rosecrans of the Rebels approach. A strong force would arrive soon, so he could not consider a surrender.

The Confederate officer nodded, then saluted. Baldwin returned the salute and watched them ride away. Then he and the sergeant returned to the stockade, where he dispatched a runner to the fort. Certainly help would have to come now.

Inside the stockade, all 50 men stood ready by the loopholes. Baldwin watched the cavalry dismount and form a skirmish line. The enemy had considerably less than two divisions in sight and no artillery, but it was more than enough manpower to overwhelm the post. Still, Baldwin didn't even consider surrender. It simply was not in his makeup to disobey an order.

The Rebel skirmish line began advancing on the stockade, and some of Baldwin's men grew anxious. He heard them cock their rifles. Their ragged breathing sounded loud in the momentary stillness that always seemed to precede battle.

"Don't fire until I order it," Baldwin called out.

Steadily forward came the gray ranks. At 200 yards, Baldwin ordered the first volley. Fifty rifles barked in unison, and gaps appeared in the Rebel front ranks. The rattle of fire swelled from both sides then. For several minutes the defenders maintained their heavy fire, then the attackers fell back out of range.

"Cease fire," Baldwin ordered. He made a hurried check and found no casualties.

Then a battery of Confederate artillery wheeled into position about 600 yards to the east. Baldwin knew that would soon end it, unless the big guns of the fort opened up or help arrived. But still he gave no thought to surrender — not while possessing the means to resist. The Rebel battery opened fire. Long tongues of flames darted from the muzzles of the cannon, ringed by clouds of smoke. The first round slashed down the flag pole and the second knocked out the center section of the east wall. The men sprawled out flat behind the dirt they had shoveled against the walls, so the shells passed over them. They raised up only to fire and the dropped back behind the dirt. But shell fragments and splinters from the logs searched them out one by one. One cannon shot came in at exactly the same time a sergeant raised up to fire. It ripped away the man's lower jaw, and his screams made even Baldwin shudder.

The barrage continued until all the stockade walls had vanished, and all but one of the 50 enlisted men lay dead or wounded. One shell fragment slashed open Baldwin's left wrist, exposing the bone.

The Confederate lines encircled the stockade now. They moved in on foot, with hardly any of the defenders able to return their fire. Baldwin knew there would be no help from the fort, and he no longer possessed the means to resist. He tied a white rag to the remains of the flag pole and raised it high. Firing faded. The battle ended 90 minutes after it had started.

General Wheeler himself led the Confederate forces to the stockade and tongue-lashed Baldwin for defending a position under such hopeless circumstances — for needless sacrifice of his men — for violating the rules of war by not surrendering earlier. Baldwin then showed the General his written orders to defend the bridge until relieved of the responsibility.

The General's fierce countenance softened a little, and he nodded to Baldwin.

"You have done more than your duty," the General commended, returning the orders to Baldwin.

Rebel medics tended to the Union wounded while other Rebs burned the bridge and destroyed or confiscated munitions, food and clothing. In minutes, nothing of value to the Union was left, and smoke from the burning trestle fouled the air, so high it must have been clearly visible to Fort Rosecrans. But still no help came. Baldwin mounted a horse provided him and rode south with the staff officers of General Wheeler. His men still able to march trailed behind, afoot. The critically wounded remained in what was left of the stockade. A couple of miles south, a staff officer offered Baldwin parole — meaning that he would be set free on his promise not to fight again unless released to do so by a similar parole of a Confederate officer.

Baldwin explained that the Union Army had recently ordered all its forces to refuse such paroles, saying such documents would not be honored by the North. Then he declined the parole. His men declined also, making Baldwin even more proud of them than he had been for their courage at the stockade. This closeness to his men would mark his nearly 40 years service in the army.

The march continued through the day, until they were at least ten miles from the fort. Then a staff officer told Baldwin he and his men were free to go back to Fort Rosecrans, without agreeing to parole. He handed Baldwin a safe conduct pass signed by General Wheeler.

Baldwin's men bore little resemblance to soldiers the next morning when they dragged into Fort Rosecrans. All but one were walking wounded or stretcher cases. But they perked up when the regimental band greeted them with lively tunes.

For his actions beyond the call of duty, Baldwin was recommended for the Medal of Honor, but the recommendation was turned down. Otherwise, his two later awards would have made him the first triple winner. Only one other would ever be recommended for a third award. Baldwin did get a promotion to captain the following March, primarily due to his actions defending the bridge.

During the Atlanta campaign of General Sherman, Baldwin helped drive General Johnston's forces from Resaca, Georgia, 13-16 May 1864; struck the retreating forces at Camilla, Georgia, 19-22 May; fought at New Hope Church, Burnt Hickory, Pumpkinville Creek and Altoona Hills between 25 May; and spent early June at Kenesaw Mountains 9 June, Golgotha 16 June and Culp's Farm 22 June. By late July, Sherman's forces rushed toward Atlanta, certain the Rebels wouldn't even try to make a serious stand there.

One of the oddities of both of Baldwin's decorations was the almost slapstick comedy at the beginning of each event. The first came at Peachtree Creek, the last natural barrier just north of Atlanta. Confederate forces had retreated across the creek and set up a line of defense in the wooded area to the south. When the Yanks caught sight of Peachtree Creek, and no Rebels, they went wild. After two months without baths or changing clothes, they couldn't stand the smell of themselves, much less each other. Down the hill they charged, 20,000 bearded and scroungy scarecrows, shedding their uniforms as they ran. Had the Rebels been able to see the creek from their new position, likely they would have fled all the way to Atlanta thinking the devil had unleashed all the banshees of hell on them.

Baldwin didn't even try to hold back his company. It would have been like trying to sop up the stream with a tea towel. By the time he reached the river, he could hardly see the water for all the naked soldiers jumping and splashing around, shouting and laughing. And when he spotted General Sherman himself, naked and squatting in the water, Baldwin, too, took his long delayed bath. Then he joined the company in boiling their filthy uniforms in thundermugs scrounged from the field hospital.

What a time for the enemy to charge! Atlanta might have been saved. "Of all the words of voice or pen, the saddest are what might have been."

The word "creek" was something of a misnomer, for the Peachtree was too deep for the army to ford; pontooniers had to build pontoon bridges at numerous points. Once they were built, the army began the crossing on the morning of 20 July 1864. Baldwin led his company across, unaware of the glory awaiting him that day, aware only of the sound of horses hooves on the wooden planing of the bridges. Likely he would have given the matter little thought, even had he known. Doing a job in a proper military manner was about all that ever concerned him.

It took most of the morning for the two corps to cross, then reassemble. Almost immediately, six lines totaling 20,000 gray-coated Confederate infantry marched out of the forest about two miles south, closing rapidly. The Confederates were through retreating. Cannons cut loose from both sides, and the Rebs charged, screaming with the choked fury and frustration accumulated in many weeks of running the other way. Only 200 yards separated the forces when the Union front ranks opened fire, with deadly results.

Unknown to Baldwin, the brigade that was supposed to be at his left flank was not there. It didn't take the Rebels long to find this weak spot and pour through it. This forced Baldwin to swing his company around and reform his line. The men couldn't load fast enough to knock down all their targets now.

Baldwin used his bloody sword to motion his company back into position on the crest of a small hill. The Confederates reformed and charged again, and again the Union line drove them back. As the Rebels withdrew, Baldwin ordered his men to charge, and he trotted down the hill well ahead of them. Then he saw two Confederate officers jump from behind a bush about 20 yards in front of him, running toward their retreating lines. One carried the guidon of his Georgia regiment. The two had fallen behind and hid in the bush, but the sight of Baldwin's force made the cover appear of doubtful value. Now, Baldwin ran full speed at them, feeling like a school boy playing a game of chase. He soon overtook the pair and jabbed each lightly with the tip of his sword.

He ordered them to halt. They did.

He ordered them down on their bellies, hands on the

backs of their heads. Down they went. Both glanced back at him, then at each other, as the angry buzz of shots from both lines seemed to reach out for Baldwin. He quickly joined them on the ground, facing them with sword at ready. For several minutes all three squirmed deeper into the soil as the bullets snarled just over their rumps. Baldwin should have been the most uncomfortable of the three, for it was only 50 yards to the Confederate lines and three times that distance to his own. But the Rebels acted as if the distance differential was of no great consequence.

"Hey, Yank," one of them called. "Wouldn't you like to be a babe in your mother's arms right about now?"

"Yeh," Baldwin answered, "a *female* babe. Then I wouldn't ever have to serve in the army."

All three chuckled at the humor, perhaps even at the absurdity of their attitudes, but none thought the situation humorous or absurd enough to raise up an inch or two and check the progress of the battle.

Finally the Confederate lines broke, heading for Atlanta and parts further south, leaving the field to the Union forces. Baldwin then marched his two prisoners back to his company, complete with their regimental colors. So unassuming was Baldwin that he didn't even report his act of valor to his superiors. But his colonel soon learned of it and summoned him to headquarters for an oral citation. He later received his first Medal of Honor for the day's service.

Baldwin went on to participate in the siege of Atlanta 28 July - 2 September, including the battle of Utvy Creek; the siege of Savannah 10-21 December; the capture of Columbia, South Carolina 16-17 February 1865; and battles at Chesterfield, South Carolina 2 March; Averysboro and Bentonville, North Carolina 15 March; and his final significant campaign 19-21 March at

Goldsboro, North Carolina. He was mustered out 10 June 1865, a 22-year-old captain.

In the reorganized post-war army, Baldwin secured a commission as a first lieutenant 23 February 1866. But his only conquest that year was the heart of Alice Blackwood, Northville, Michigan. He had met Alice two years earlier at a seminary for young women in Albion, Michigan, while visiting his sister there. They were married 10 January 1867. For a honeymoon they traveled to his new regiment, the 38th Infantry, at distant Fort Harker, Kansas.

Baldwin enjoyed soldiering on the frontier, but not the rough life for Alice. That year at Fort Harker set the pattern for most of their years at isolated posts in the west — crude housing; few, if any, female companions; bitter winters and blistering summers; few comforts of civilization. But Alice cared less about this than did Frank. She never asked for more than to be near her husband, sharing the only life that interested him.

The Baldwins survived both the vicious weather and a cholera epidemic that winter of 1866-67, then left for an even more remote post in New Mexico the following September. It was the worst possible time to go, because Alice was nearly eight months pregnant. An overland journey by covered wagon with her that far along could have been fatal. Fear touched Frank for the first time in his life. But Alice insisted on making the trip with him rather than going back east until after the baby was born. Their only child, Juanita Mary, was born 12 October 1867, in their covered wagon near Trinidad, Colorado, enroute to New Mexico.

The Baldwins spent more than a year in New Mexico, then returned to Kansas in 1869. Next came duty in Michigan and Kentucky. Frank joined the command of Colonel Nelson A. Miles in 1874, at Fort Dodge, Kansas. This last step was significant; he would serve with Miles, who recognized his rare talents and helped him professionally, for many years. The two were to become lifelong friends, as well. Also, he joined the Colonel in time for the 1874-5 campaign against the Kiowas and Comanches in Indian Territory, critical months in his life.

The expedition left 31 July with two battalions of cavalry, four companies of infantry and an artillery detachment. Baldwin soon became a favorite of Miles, because he was the most dependable officer in the Fifth Infantry. He commanded the company of scouts — Delaware Indians, soldiers, and such civilian scouts as Billy Dixon and Bat Masterson — riding point throughout the long campaign.

The first important skirmish came 30 August 1874, on the Salt Fork of the Red River. Baldwin kept his scouts several miles in front of the main command. Just ahead, the Red River spilled down through rocky bluffs. Nothing seemed amiss to him, so he rode up to the cliffs. The small detachment must have appeared an easy target to the hostiles waiting at the top of the bluff. They charged down the slopes with wild war cries, firing as they rode.

Baldwin plunged from his saddle and yelled at the scouts to do the same. The order wasn't really needed. Baldwin worked along behind the line, directing them into a skirmish line and correcting their fire. The heavy blast of their rifles would warn Colonel Miles, so Baldwin didn't bother to send back word of the ambush. He kept his men in a tight skirmish formation, too busy to think of much else.

The scouts cut down the first line of attackers, if attacking Indians can be described as a line, and Baldwin pulled the left flank up a little to produce a better concentration of fire power. As more hostiles came down the slope, Baldwin ordered his men forward, catching the

Indians off balance despite their superiority in numbers, and driving them back. Then he heard the sound of bugles. Battalions charged in on both sides, crushing the ambushers. In moments the Indians fled across the broken country, with the mounted infantry and cavalry just behind.

At first the hostiles stopped periodically to fight, but each time the troopers smashed directly into them. Only the scorching heat and arid land kept the troopers from a greater victory; they eventually had to return to their wagons for water and supplies. For his part in the skirmish and pursuit, Baldwin received the brevet rank of captain.

The pursuit of various Kiowa and Comanche bands continued through September and October and into icy November on the staked plains — country so desolate that trails across it had to be marked with poles driven into the ground; otherwise, travelers might wander around in circles and leave the area.

By November, even the supply wagons were empty. Baldwin commanded a detachment ordered back to the supply base on the Washita River. A company of infantry, a troop of cavalry, one mountain howitzer and three empty wagons pulled by six-mule teams made up the "non-combatant" mission. The sole mission of the cavalry and infantry was to protect the wagons.

Baldwin's detachment pulled out about 10 p.m., 4 November 1874, hoping the cover of darkness would give them some measure of protection. His detachment wasn't large enough to withstand a determined attack by even a small war party.

For three days the detachment traveled northeast, using all the natural cover Baldwin could find — gullies, river beds, and wooded areas. After dark on the third day, he called a halt in a cottonwood grove on the banks of McClellan's Creek, Texas. Only one who has felt the dagger-thrust of icy west Texas winds can appreciate how cold the men were that night. But Baldwin dared only let them light tiny fires, just long enough to heat some coffee. Even this concession to comfort was risky, as the next morning would soon prove.

Long before daylight, Baldwin sent scouts out north and east. He allowed the troops to make coffee again, with great reluctance. He could feel trouble but couldn't see visible signs of it.

Just as Baldwin started the command on the trail, he spotted one of his scouts galloping in at rash speed. The scout reined in, caught his breath, and reported finding a large hostile camp about a mile ahead, just beyond a ridge. He had recognized the tepee of Grey Beard, a Cheyenne chief. Had the camp been any other, Baldwin likely would have sent for help before attacking the superior force; but Grey Beard held two small white girls captive, girls long sought by the army. To delay would mean the escape of Grey Beard and perhaps death for the girls. So Baldwin sent the scout to Colonel Miles with word that he was attacking the camp.

Baldwin immediately led the train toward the ridge screening the hostiles. He halted at the ridge top and looked down through the pre-dawn grayness at the camp still asleep and partially hidden in a grove of cottonwoods very much like the one the command had just left. A line of tepees followed the snake track of the icy creek. Baldwin figured there were about a hundred lodges, perhaps 300 warriors, three-to-one odds against him. He knew it would be rash to attack with a single troop of cavalry and a company of infantry, and rashness was not one of his traits. But the two girls had been sought for months by the army, and that made attack his duty.

Then Baldwin dreamed up a bit of trickery that would

add to the element of surprise, later win him a second Medal of Honor, and give the army something to chuckle about in future years. He ordered both cavalry and wagons "front into line" for a charge, with the infantry-laden wagons and his howitzer in the center and the cavalry on the flanks. To the wagonmaster he said, "Once the charge starts, you'll have to keep up. There won't be anyone to protect you." The wagonmaster nodded his understanding. Then Baldwin rode out front of the line a few yards and glanced back at his unlikely looking attack force. Perhaps he wondered if anyone would ever believe his plan.

Baldwin waved at his bugler who immediately shattered the quiet morning by sounding the charge. Baldwin dug in his spurs and sent his mount hurtling down the slope. From the line behind him came enough screaming and yelling for a force many times its size — at least, he hoped the Cheyenne would think so. The Indians tumbled half naked out of their tepees as the first shots snarled at them. What a sight it must have been to them. Charging cavalry they knew quite well, but onrushing wagons with riflemen blazing away and a cannon bounding down the slopes, despite the fact that it was useless while in motion, terrified them. They scattered to the west.

Baldwin ordered the men nearest him to shoot any Indian trying to reach the tepee of Grey Beard. That's where the girls would be, and Indians usually killed white captives when under attack.

On through the camp went the charge, knocking over tepees and driving all Indians to the west. The warriors formed a shield to permit their families time to escape, but the howitzer soon routed them again. For four hours the cavalry and wagons charged, re-formed, charged, and re-formed, driving the hostiles twelve miles before they were so scattered that further pursuit was useless.

Back in the camp the Germaine sisters, Adelaide, 7, and Julia, 5, had been found under a buffalo robe in the tepee of Grey Beard. Baldwin had never seen such filthy, emaciated children. Nearly starved, clad in stinking rags, their legs raw from riding Indian ponies bareback, the girls drew back from them in terror until they learned the men were soldiers. They had heard their two older sisters — captured at the same time they were — praying for soldiers to rescue them. The older girls, now with another band of Cheyenne, were freed the next year.

For his daring at McClellan's Creek, Lieutenant Baldwin received his second Medal of Honor.

The Fifth Infantry kept up the pressure through the winter of 1874-5, driving various bands of Kiowa, Comanche, Arapaho and Cheyenne from their winter encampments. The pressure eventually drove the hostiles to their reservations to avoid starvation and freezing.

In 1875, the Fifth Infantry made a quick trip to New Mexico when Utes and Apaches threatened to jump their reservations. Then 33, Baldwin was still only a lieutenant — except for brevet rank — in an era when promotions only occurred when a higher ranking officer in the regiment died or retired. But he remained the top officer for Colonel Miles — his most dependable — receiving assignments Miles dared not trust to most of his underlings. Baldwin led patrols that found no indication of hostiles off their reservations, so the command returned to Fort Leavenworth, Kansas, in December.

The Custer massacre in June 1876, brought cavalry and infantry pouring into Sioux country to satisfy an outraged public. The mighty camp that had destroyed the Seventh Cavalry had split into many smaller bands and scattered. The Fifth Infantry arrived in July and engaged in a long pursuit; in October it caught up with Sitting Bull's main camp. An all-day skirmish followed, then flight by the

Indians. The Fifth extended pursuit, but the mounted Sioux had little trouble keeping ahead of walking infantry. Miles then divided his command into three columns, one — a battalion of 106 officers and men — under Baldwin. This, alone, showed how much confidence Miles had in the junior officer who had distinguished himself against the southern plains tribes.

With mule-drawn supply wagons and only four riding mounts, Frank marched off in late October as winter squeezed in on Montana. Temperatures remained well below zero and two feet of snow obscured the rugged country. The mules began to drop, and the men weakened in the fierce weather. But Baldwin remained on the march. Only tenacity would allow them to prevail over the swift moving Sioux and Cheyenne. His scouts finally located Sitting Bull's camp 7 December, on the Missouri River in Montana.

Baldwin wanted to move faster than the supply wagons could traverse the rough country, so he ordered five days' rations issued each man. They marched out within an hour of learning the location of the camp. The infantry trudged for hours across the frozen country, making camp after dark. The Sioux camp lay only a few miles further, but Baldwin decided to wait for morning to attack.

Sitting Bull knew Baldwin's command was there, however, and — with a six-to-one edge — spent the night fortifying his position.

When Baldwin marched up the next morning, he found a position too strong to attack. Sitting Bull motioned him away, and Baldwin simply withdrew to fight another day. The Sioux pulled out later in the day and Baldwin followed.

A few days later the Sioux crossed to the south side of the Missouri River, then spread out in a skirmish line around the ford. It appeared Sitting Bull was tired of

Baldwin's command dogging his trail; but Baldwin, long wise to Indian traps, approached the ford cautiously. The Sioux opened fire across the river, then soon withdrew into the badlands.

Again Baldwin followed. This type of pursuit, during the winter months when the Indians like to hole up, proved to be as discouraging to the Sioux as it had been to the southern plains tribes. It took its toll on Baldwin's force also. Men and mules simply "wore out" during the extended march. For days they saw nothing but frozen snow. Rations had to be cut. Mules lived on what few tree branches they could forage. But the tenacity paid off 18 December when Sitting Bull encamped on the Red Water without knowing the nearness of Baldwin's force. The entire pursuit had been directed toward just such a moment, when surprise would offset the superior size of the Sioux band. On a ridge overlooking the camp, Baldwin turned to his starving men.

"Down there is all the buffalo meat you can eat," he told them. Nothing else needed to be said. They hurried into a line just behind the ridgecrest. Baldwin repeated his tactics of McClellan's Creek by putting his wagons into the line. When the wagons came bouncing down the hillside, with screaming infantry running alongside, Sitting Bull's warriors fled. Perhaps they thought the wagons were field pieces, the one thing they feared above all else.

The infantry, too weak to pursue, collected the Indians' horses and mules, then gorged themselves on roast buffalo meat. That was the first warm night and full belly they had known in weeks. The next day they destroyed the lodges and took the food, clothing and animals back to the cantonment on Tongue River.

Although Sitting Bull escaped, the loss of his village left his people at the mercy of the savage winter, without food or shelter, or the means to get either. Many died.

Many others sullenly trudged into the Sioux reservation. Sitting Bull and a small segment of his people eventually fled to Canada.

For his courage and tactics, Baldwin was breveted with the rank of major, although still a first lieutenant for pay purposes.

The men had hardly thawed out before a band of Cheyenne, allied with the Sioux of Crazy Horse, precipitated another march by raiding the regimental cattle herd, stealing 250 head. The desperate measure could only mean the hostiles were starving. Colonel Miles took 436 men on the rail immediately, with Baldwin commanding the scouts. Temperatures ranged from zero to thirty below, the snow from one to four feet, the terrain from bad to worse. After several days, a thaw brought rain and mud. Then the slashing cold and snow returned. Sometimes they marched only three or four miles in a full day. But march they did, along the rugged valley of the Tongue River, crossing it and its tributaries dozens of times. Several times they encountered a few hostiles, or hastily abandoned camps.

Nearly two weeks after taking to the trail, Baldwin's scouts found a recent campsite more than a mile long — a big band. The next day, 6 January 1877, started with a snowstorm but the regiment marched 15 miles anyway. They crossed rivers three times 7 January before camping in the midst of the Wolf Mountains. On nearby hilltops, Indians stood in the open watching them. The main band was nearby, then, and through running. An attack would come next morning.

With the dawn, the infantry deployed across the valley in a skirmish line. Baldwin rode along the line calling out encouragement.

"They'll charge soon," he said. "Be ready. Stand fast. They can't break through a firm line of infantry."

The attack came about 7 a.m., a massive head-on charge up the valley into the ready rifles and two artillery pieces. The first volley of rifle and cannon fire blew away the charge. Fading into the rocks and trees, the hostiles sniped at the infantry while surrounding it. Baldwin spotted one group working up a hill on the left — a key position if they reached the top. He pointed this out to Colonel Miles, who sent two companies hurrying up the near side. The infantry drove them off, but the hostiles topped another bluff from which they could fire down on the infantry struggling up the steep slope.

For more than an hour, the soldiers fought upward slowly. Then Baldwin realized they were firing less and less. They must be running out of ammunition. He mounted his horse and placed a box of rifle ammunition on the saddle in front of him, then spurred the mount toward the hill. Up the slope he rode, acutely aware of the whine of bullets around him. He reached the men and handed down the box. As soon as they reloaded their weapons, he spurred on up the slope waving his hat and yelling for the men to follow him. They did, as men in the ranks generally do when inspired by such an example.

As Baldwin approached the rim he paused for a moment, not quite believing what he saw. An Indian, apparently a medicine chief, jumped up and started dancing along the rim of the bluff, in clear sight of the troops. Bright red, blue and yellow feathers adorned his blanket and war bonnet, and Baldwin could hear tiny bells tinkling from his moccasins. The Indian apparently wanted to show the braves that his medicine was too powerful for the soldiers' bullets. He danced 40 or 50 yards without a shot fired at him by the astonished soldiers. Then he danced back. Scattered rifle shots searched for him, missing at first, then tumbling him into the snow.

The soldiers yelled in unison and scrambled on up and

over the rim. Panicked by the loss of the medicine man, the Indians scattered back to the main body. Then all of them fled up the valley, ending the battle of Wolf Mountain.

Once again Baldwin was cited in Colonel Miles' report. But this time he paid the price of catching a lung ailment that would plague him for many years.

As soon as he recovered, at least temporarily, Baldwin returned to duty. He rode on the 1877 expedition against the Sioux of Lame Deer and remained in the field almost continuously for the next three years. His permanent promotion to captain came in 1879. Then frigid winters finally did what the hostile Indians could not. His recurring lung ailment forced him to take sick leave in 1880. He and Alice toured Europe while he recuperated.

Baldwin returned to active service in 1881, for four years as judge advocate, Department of the Columbia, Washington Territory. His old commander, Nelson A. Miles, now a general, commanded the department. From 1885 to 1891, Baldwin served in the field with his regiment, all over the great plains. Then came three years duty as inspector of small arms practice, Department of the Missouri, Chicago, followed by four years as Indian agent, Anadarko, Indian Territory.

At the age of 56, Baldwin should have been willing to sit out the Spanish-American War. But the habits of 37 years were too strong. He accepted a promotion to major, requesting and getting duty in Cuba.

Still another — and final — campaign remained for the old soldier, in the Philippine Insurrection immediately following the Spanish surrender. Now a lieutenant colonel, he requested transfer to the Philippines because that was where the action was. He took command of the Fourth Infantry at Cavite, Luzon Island 26 May 1900. Cavite Province was the heart of the insurrection movement, and Baldwin took on the task of clearing the area of rebels. He proceeded in the same methodical manner he had used against the plains Indians for so many years. His men pursued and harassed the Rebels until they could get no rest, no time to regroup or to heal their wounds. Months of this brought the surrender of General Trias and 2,000 insurrectors, ending the struggle in Cavite Province. Citations for his service included one from President Theodore Roosevelt and earned him a promotion to full colonel in 1901.

Colonel Baldwin was the ideal commander for the final significant battle of the campaign 2 May 1902, on Mindanao, largest island in the Philippines. He commanded the 27th Infantry stationed on the coast. Savage Moros had always controlled the island except for small pockets on the coast. Now they blockaded every trail leading inland. Exploring parties sent to the interior could travel only short distances before Moros routed them. Baldwin learned their stronghold was a fortress overlooking Lake Lanao somewhere in the unknown interior. What a challenge to the old warrior. He learned roughly where the lake was located, then organized an expedition and set out for the legendary lake.

During the difficult march inland he must have thought often of his campaigns on the staked plains of Texas and the badlands of Montana. The Moros sniped at them frequently each day, chopped down trees and piled up entanglements of thorn bushes and vines to block the trail. But the old war horse had known too many equally rugged marches. While some of his men kept the snipers at a distance, others cleared the trail. Most of the soldiers were youngsters, but they didn't outmarch the Colonel, nor outfight him.

The infantry reached Lake Lanao 2 May, and Baldwin thought it one of the beauty spots of the world, unspoiled by civilization. But he was more interested in the tactical situation of the fortress overlooking the lake. The dirt, logs and stone walls offered no problems that disciplined troops couldn't handle. He ordered an immediate attack. The Moros fought with their legendary tenacity, a trait Baldwin could appreciate better than most, but well-trained soldiers and rapid fire weapons soon drove from the fortress all those still alive. Baldwin had 51 dead and 472 wounded. The victory earned him a brigadier general's star the following month.

The mandatory retirement age of 64 caught Baldwin in 1906, and he settled down for his twilight years in Denver. Honors came his way, among them an honorary doctor of law degree from his old school, Hillsdale College of Michigan. He also served as adjutant general for Colorado during World War I.

General Frank Dwight Baldwin died 22 April 1923, in Denver, at the age of 80 years and 10 months. He is buried in Arlington National Cemetery on the Potomac River.

FOURTH DOUBLE WINNER Capt. Frank Baldwin.

FOURTH DOUBLE WINNER Capt. Frank Baldwin (center, white trousers) is shown with officers and men at Fort Davis, Texas, about 1888. Famed Civil War and Indian Wars leader General Grierson (seated, left center) is shown in civilian clothes and hat. Others are unknown.

An artist's conception of Capt. Frank Baldwin earning his SECOND MEDAL OF HONOR with his wagon attack on Grey Beard's band at McClellan's Creek, Texas, 8 November 1874.

CHAPTER FIVE

Patrick Leonard (?-?)

Only three U.S. Army enlisted men ever received two Medals of Honor, all six being earned during the Indian Wars of the 1870s. The three sergeants were typical of the frontier army noncoms: tough, hard, tenacious. Two of the three — including Patrick Leonard — were among the many Irish emigrants who helped fill the ranks of the old army.

Leonard liked to fight, in barrooms, behind the barracks, anywhere. Minor skirmishes with Indians in Nebraska provided him the opportunity to use this talent to win his Medals of Honor.

The skimpy records now available include very little else about the scrappy Irishman.

In May 1870, Leonard was C Troop sergeant in the Second U.S. Cavalry, protecting settlers scattered along the Little Blue River and its tributaries, particularly Spring Creek, in south central Nebraska. For several weeks the company camped on the south banks of the little Blue River, sending out daily patrols over the area.

Leonard found the duty rather dull because that area of Nebraska was dead quiet that spring — until mid-May. Unknown to the troop, a hundred hostile Cheyenne moved into the area with the intention of killing or driving off all the settlers in the area.

A routine patrol left camp 13 May 1870. Two of the troopers returned early 15 May, looking for two horses that had broken loose. They had lost the trail in the area of Spring Creek, about seven miles away. Captain E. J. Spaulding, troop commander, detailed Sergeant Leonard and four privates to ride along Spring Creek, follow it to the last settlement, and return to camp.

No one yet knew of the hostiles in the area. The brief ride would be a break in the monotony. Leonard rode out with the four privates at a brisk gait. At Spring Creek they found two wagons and five civilian surveyors. None of them had seen the missing horses, so Leonard pushed on upstream toward the settlement. About 10 a.m., he spotted a band of horsemen about four miles away. Assuming the party was Lieutenant Fowler's patrol, he spurred his mount to a faster gait to catch up. The distant horsemen vanished in a wooded area somewhat away from the creek. Leonard increased his gait and passed through the woods to a clearing beyond. He hardly noticed ravines on each side, well-removed from the trail, until 50 Indians rode up out of them with piercing whoops and booming rifles.

What a feeling that must have been for the five troopers, caught between the two onrushing hostile groups. The normal reaction would have been to run. Some of the five might even have made it. But Leonard never considered the possibility. As the hostile groups galloped in, the troopers reined up.

"Dismount," Leonard ordered, stepping from the saddle.

Although the Indians fired their rifles from galloping horses, they didn't shoot wild. One bullet broke the wrist of Private Hubbard Thomas of Philadelphia. Others wounded two horses. Leonard immediately made the wounded Thomas the horseholder by passing him his reins. The others did likewise.

Leonard and Private George W. Thompson of Victory, New York, kneeled on the left side and opened fire with their carbines. Private Heth Canfield of New Medford, Connecticut, and Michael Himmelsback of Allegheny County, Pennsylvania, took the right side. Their blistering fire emptied four saddles quickly and drove the Indians back to the ravines, taking their casualties with them. A few pickets watched over the edges of the ravines, but most of the Indians kept out of sight for several minutes.

In the manner of the professional soldier, Leonard used the minutes to advantage. He led one of the wounded horses around to the right side of the trail, drew his revolver and shot the mount in the brain. The horse fell where Leonard had anticipated, forming a breastwork against attack from that side. Then he led the other wounded mount around to the south side and shot it also.

Keep low, he warned his troopers, and all of them stretched out behind the dead horses. The wounded Thomas stretched out on his back, still holding the reins of the horses with one hand but letting the reins out as far as they would go.

"Reckon they'll be back?" Thompson asked.

Leonard ignored the question, knowing no answer was expected.

The second charge came quickly enough, anyway. The Indians galloped up out of the ravines, firing as they came and yelping in that curious high-pitched manner so unnerving to most whites of that period.

The troopers fired, loaded, and fired their carbines again with well-trained speed, killing two more hostiles and severely wounding four others who remained in their saddles only with the help of other warriors riding alongside them. The hostiles took refuge in the ravines again, this time for half an hour. Then a dozen or so of the Indians rode off with their dead and wounded. The rest, about 40, began riding in a circle around the defensive position but just out of effective carbine range. Occasionally a small number of them would make a feint toward the soldiers, an old warrior trick to make defenders waste ammunition. But Leonard cautioned his men to hold their fire.

Some of the riders dropped to the ground and crept in close enough to snipe at the soldiers, but the breastwork of dead mounts nullified their efforts. However, they did kill the other three cavalry horses. This proved important half an hour later when the troopers loaded their last cartridges in their carbines. When one of the horses was shot, it staggered off about 20 feet before it dropped dead. Tied to its saddle was a full cartridge box.

"We've got to have that box," Leonard said. "Cover me."

The other three fired at the nearest snipers while Leonard jumped up and ran toward the dead horse. He pulled a knife from his belt and slashed the leather cords holding the box to the saddle. A bullet hit the dirt inches from his right boot, perhaps giving him a little extra speed returning to the breastwork with the much needed ammo.

The desultory sniping and feinting continued another hour without further casualties. A stand-off of this sort never appealed much to any of the plains Indians. They withdrew.

The safe thing for Leonard to do was hurry back to the troop camp and warn the captain of the hostiles in the area. Unknown to him, most of the command was already searching for the Indians because a settler had been killed five miles south of the camp and horses had been stolen from several farms. Leonard decided it was more important to warn the settlers two miles on up the creek from the ambush site, so he marched his men toward the settlement. Here he found two women and a child alone. The man of the house was gone.

Taking the settlers with him, Leonard started out for the lower settlement on Spring Creek. They walked only one mile before 40 Indians — probably the same group — surrounded them just out of carbine range. Before the Indians could attack, the two wagons of civilian surveyors lumbered into sight, so the hostiles pulled back a little. Leonard waited until the wagons reached his group, then joined them and marched on. The Indians hovered nearby, ahead and to the left but out of firing range, until dark. Then they vanished.

Shortly after 10 p.m., Leonard led his weary party into the troop camp. Captain Spaulding rode in about an hour later and immediately left with a force large enough to attack the hostile band. He never found them.

Leonard and the four privates received Medals of Honor for their valor.

Little is known of Leonard during the next six years, except that sometime during that period he did something rare for a cavalryman — he transferred or *was* transferred to the infantry. Considering the contempt the groundpounders and horse soldiers of that period had for each other, it is difficult to imagine Leonard making the change voluntarily. Also, Leonard dropped in rank to corporal. Available records don't show why either of these things happened, but his Irish temper offers a strong possibility.

April of 1876, found Corporal Leonard with Company A, 23rd Infantry, at Fort Hartsuff, Nebraska, about 200 miles west of Omaha. Built on the Loup River in 1874, to protect settlers against Sioux raids, it wasn't a fort in the usual sense, for it had no walls around its buildings. A small stockade on a hilltop overlooking the rest of the structures was its only fortification.

The Sioux regarded the Loup Valley as their hunting grounds and also had to pass through it to raid their hereditary enemies, the Pawnees. So, Fort Hartsuff irritated them more than many outposts. Despite this, and the fact that only a single company manned the post, the Sioux never attacked it. Perhaps it was because they were too busy with Custer, Miles and Terry during the brief span of Hartsuff's existence.

Company A had manned the post about a year when a minor incident occurred 28 April 1876. Six hostile Sioux rode down the valley, probably on a horse stealing or scalp hunting expedition. By traveling at night, the raiders avoided detection until they were only a few miles north of the fort. Early in the morning, a settler galloped into the fort seeking help. Volunteers for the relief mission included Lieutenant Charles H. Heyl of Philadelphia, a Sergeant Daugherty, Corporal Jeptha L. Lytton of Lawrence County, Indiana, six privates, and, quite naturally, Patrick Leonard.

The detachment rode out of the fort about 8 a.m. as mounted infantry, which must have pleased an old yellowleg like Leonard. At a full gallop the detail quickly reached the area where the raiders had been spotted. An excited farmer told them a group of settlers had chased the Sioux on north. The detail followed.

The country changed from farm land to sandhills, formed by silt that had once been the ocean floor. This slowed the tiring mounts which kicked up choking dust. Twenty-five miles north of the fort, they found the settlers behind a low sandhill. The Sioux were in a blowout, a bowl-shaped hole about 30 feet across blown in the gentle slope of another sandhill nearby. The settlers had the Sioux at bay but lacked the courage to finish the job. All refused to help the soldiers.

Lieutenant Heyl sent the six privates around to the far side of the sandhill to cut off escape. They moved in a wide circle, in case the hidden Sioux should decide to look over the edge of the blowout. To the Lieutenant, an easterner ignorant in the ways of Indian fighting, those in the crater seemed harmless enough. He couldn't even see any of the Indians, and certainly only six of the savages couldn't be much of a menace. His only worry was that the Indians might escape. He turned to his three remaining men, Sergeant Daugherty, Corporal Lytton and Corporal Leonard.

"We'll give them a few more minutes to get in position, then we'll charge from this side," Heyl said. "If the hostiles show any sign of resistance, we'll have to shoot them. But most likely they are hoping for the chance to surrender."

How Leonard must have been startled at that evaluation. He knew that cornered Sioux could be real bearcats. But the rashness of the plan likely appealed to him anyway. What little is known of his character certainly indicates as much.

At the Lieutenant's signal, the four of them ran across the clearing and up the slope. Fortunately, none of the Sioux peered over the lip of the crater. When Leonard climbed high enough to see inside the depression, the Sioux were hunkered well away from the edge, in a powwow. They spotted Leonard at the same moment and sprawled out prone, bringing rifles into position. The blast of longguns rocked the hillside. A slug aimed at Leonard knocked sand from the lip of the crater almost directly in front of him. He fired at a prone figure until he saw the Indian roll over, then picked a new target. The shooting lasted only seconds, though it likely seemed much longer. Then the Lieutenant ordered a retreat. Sergeant Daugherty lay near Leonard, dead or unconscious. Leonard and Lytton grabbed the Sergeant by the arms and dragged him back to cover, but the Sergeant was dead.

At least three of the Sioux had been hit, so the Lieutenant decided he and the two corporals should charge again and finish the job. But Leonard and Lytton protested in most unmilitary fashion.

"The Indians would be ready this time," Leonard said. They wouldn't get ten feet. "What would you suggest?" the Lieutenant asked.

Leonard pointed to some scattered rocks and sand knots. They could work up closer, and each time Indians stuck up their heads the troopers could shoot. If that didn't get them, they could crawl up early in the morning, while it was still dark, timing it to arrive at the edge at first light.

Heyl didn't like the idea much but reluctantly gave in to the noncoms. He got one of the settlers to carry word to the six privates on the other side. Then he and the corporals darted to cover closer to the crater and sniped at the Sioux until dark. They took turns at guard duty that night, but the Sioux didn't show themselves.

Near dawn they crawled up to the edge of the blowout. It was empty. Tracks showed the Sioux had gone out the other side, past the six privates supposedly guarding that route, taking their dead and wounded with them.

The troopers took Sergeant Daugherty back to Fort Hartsuff for burial. Three weeks later, word came from the Rosebud Indian Agency in the Dakotas that three weary, almost naked, Sioux had arrived there afoot. Never again did the Sioux raid in the Loup Valley.

Leonard received his second Medal of Honor for the skirmish, but little recognition outside his own outfit. He remained unknown for most of a century, until a small U.S. Army post in Germany was named Camp Leonard.

CHAPTER SIX

William Wilson
(?-?)

Sergeant William Wilson of Philadelphia earned his two Medals of Honor with deeds only six months apart, while serving in the Fourth U.S. Cavalry of the renowned Colonel (later General) Ranald S. Mackenzie. A native of Philadelphia, he enlisted in the regiment in October 1865.

Solid and dependable, he displayed enough boldness for promotion to cavalry sergeant within six years, no easy feat in those post Civil War years of severely restricted funds for the military. In combat, his dashing tactics earned him the admiration of Mackenzie, who didn't impress easily. In fact, Mackenzie allowed Wilson to command patrols, a duty normally limited to a commissioned officer.

In 1872, Wilson's Troop I operated out of Fort Concho, Texas, near the present city of San Angelo and in the middle of a line of forts curving from Mexico to Oklahoma across the southwestern Texas frontier. The army patrolled from these posts, protecting settlers against the southern plains tribes, particularly the Comanches.

Traders known as Comancheros kept the hostiles well supplied with weapons and ammunition. Army patrols searched constantly for both raiders and traders, sometimes pursuing them across the Mexico border in violation of treaties with Mexico.

Just after reveille 12 March 1872, a frantic settler staggered into Fort Concho with word of an Indian raid on cattle in the vicinity. Sergeant Wilson left immediately with a corporal and 20 privates. He found the trail of the stolen cattle and followed it all day northwestward. About mid-afternoon he permitted a brief halt for cold food, then pushed on. Bright moonlight made it possible to follow the broad trail most of the night. Only when the moon vanished about three in the morning did he permit the men to halt for sleep.

First light roused Wilson two hours later. He ordered the bone-weary, groaning detail to saddles without even having coffee. For two hours he rode hard, finally stopping for breakfast on the south banks of the Colorado River. He sent a private up a hill to the left to stand lookout. When the private reached the top he stared upstream for just a moment then whirled around.

"Indians," he shouted, and scrambled down the hill. The raider camp lay two miles upstream.

"Hit leather," Wilson ordered, and 22 sore bottoms smacked saddles. He ordered the detail forward at a gallop.

What the trooper saw two miles away isn't known, but it wasn't the enemy; they were a lot closer. The detail had hardly started before a single rifle shot barked at them, off to the left where a small creek emptied into the Colorado River. Trees along the creek screened the raider camp from which 50 rifles now snarled at the detail. Discretion called for swift retirement from the field. Instead, Wilson spurred his mount around the campsite and up a bluff behind the raiders. The detail arrived just behind him.

From this higher position, the troopers poured a heavy and effective fire down on the raiders below, driving them to what little cover they could find. Wilson worked the lever on his carbine mechanically, surprised to see a scattering of Mexican sombreros among the Indians. The raiders must have been meeting the Comancheros. Wilson shot down one Mexican trying to mount a terrified horse, but the slight form bounded up again and chased into the brush after the horse. Wilson emptied his carbine at him, without apparent effect. He reloaded and picked off an Indian behind a skinny tree, as the last raider fled across the creek and the firing stopped.

Though none of his men was wounded, Wilson didn't pursue with his exhausted mounts. Wearily, he lumbered down the side of the bluff to the camp. Four dead Indians sprawled where they had fallen. Supplies and equipment dotted the campsite. The raiders had escaped only with their lives and the ponies they were riding.

A rustling behind a bush attracted Wilson. He pushed the limbs aside with his carbine to find a Mexican boy barely in his teens, cowering, arms raised in surrender. Wilson turned him over to one of the men. He ordered everything in the camp burned.

The detail returned to Fort Concho from the 120-mile round trip, 52 hours after leaving it.

The young Mexican boy turned out to be a real prize. When questioned, he spilled out a story in broken English of far greater significance than he realized. The Comanches came from New Mexico, he said, with guns, shells and whiskey supplied by New Mexican traders. Only the day before, the Comanches had traded their goods for the herd of stolen cattle and started home across the *Llano Estacado.*

Wilson grunted in disbelief at the name of *Llano Estacado* — the barren, staked plains. Rising 2,400 feet above sea level, the vast plains — the largest flat area in the United States — covered the eastern part of New Mexico and most of the Texas panhandle. The lack of known water and graze discouraged the army from pursuing Indians into the wasteland. Even the Indians shunned most of it. The white men drove stakes in the ground to mark the few trails used.

The Mexican boy insisted the traders regularly used a route leading from one small water hole and grass patch to the next. Several Indian camps also were scattered along the route, he claimed. He named his employer and other traders, locations of their posts in New Mexico, and explained the various means the gunrunners used to rendezvous with the marauders. The vast operation was intricate and well planned.

It didn't take much thought for Wilson to realize the fantastic importance of the information. If accurate, it would enable the army to cut the flow of weapons and ammunition to the hostiles and force them onto the Fort Sill Reservation.

The army also recognized the significance of Wilson's patrol that day, awarding him his first Medal of Honor, probably as much for securing the information as for his valor in leading the attack against a vastly superior force.

In June, Wilson's I Troop was one of five brought together from four forts by Colonel Mackenzie for a march across the staked plains. The Mexican boy guided them to the beginning of a well-marked trail leading northwestward, into what appeared to Wilson to be another world; not a living thing could be seen in any direction. The empty land lay flat and silent. The heat searing his body seemed unreal.

For twelve days, the Mexican boy led them across the desolate country, finding just enough water and grass to keep them going when added to what they carried with them. The trail took them all the way to New Mexico before it split into numerous smaller trails, and still there was no sign of Comanche or Comanchero. Apparently Wilson's victory in March had warned off the traders.

The command circled around and returned to the supply camp 30 days after leaving it, having traveled 640 miles. Although no quarry was found, the trail was no longer secret and the army could close it now. The march also proved the army could pursue hostiles into the staked plains and survive. This prompted a second expedition into the silent country, but for a different purpose.

Various tribes on the southern plains were by this time on the Fort Sill Reservation in what is now southwestern Oklahoma — at the eastern edge of the staked plains — but not the Quohadi Comanches. When pursuit got too hot, the Quohadi simply vanished into the staked plains and the army dared not follow; but no longer would this be true.

The mudholes and springs suitable for use when crossing the staked plains would not sustain large Indian encampments for long periods. From findings on various expeditions, the army now knew where to locate the year-round creeks and rivers. Mackenzie was determined to check them until he found the Quohadi. In September 1872, he challenged the staked plains again. Leaving his infantry to guard his base camp, he marched into the northwestern part of Texas with five troops of cavalry — seven officers and 215 enlisted men — and 20 Tonkawa scouts.

Despite his recent acquisition of a Medal of Honor, Sergeant Wilson was just another noncom in the field force, eating dust, leading his troop and following orders. In the manner of a professional soldier, he wanted it that way. Neither proud nor modest, he blended in well with the frontier soldiers who eventually defeated what one general called the finest light cavalry in the world — the old west Indians.

The first few days of the march appeared much like the earlier trek across the staked plains, with no sign of life, but the heat seemed less severe than back in June. Only one meal a day was allowed, about noon, and Wilson had to watch his men constantly to keep them from emptying their canteens too quickly after each water hole. They never knew when they would find another mud hole even good enough for the animals.

The cavalry began 29 September much the same as the previous eight days, marching with the first light. The usual monotony prevailed through the morning, lulling the troopers into a bored looseness in their saddles. About noon the command reached McClellan Creek, at a point about four miles upstream from where it emptied into the North Fork of the Red River. This was the same McClellan Creek where Lieutenant Frank Baldwin would earn his second Medal of Honor two years later.

From McClellan Creek, the troopers marched two miles southwest along the stream. About 1 p.m., the scouts found two fresh trails, one of two horses and one of a mule. Plains Indians had a weakness for mules, so Mackenzie gambled on following the mule trail. The command moved on along the creek bed at a fast gait. Four miles later, the trail vanished.

Another weakness of the plains Indians betrayed them at this point — a weakness for wild grapes. Captain Wirt David of F Troop spotted some grape vines growing along the stream bed on the opposite side of the stream. David rode over to investigate. Grapes lay on the ground, indicating someone had been picking them. David followed a trail of dropped grapes a short distance until he found the mule tracks again. The troops resumed hard pursuit.

The trail led northeast, angling across the V-shaped neck of land formed by McClellan Creek emptying into the North Fork of the Red River. The troops pushed their mounts for twelve miles before halting in trees along a hilltop. Four miles below, in a beautiful valley, a Comanche camp sprawled along the banks of a stream. The woods protected the soldiers from discovery, so Mackenzie ordered a breather for the tired men and mounts.

Sergeant Wilson groaned with relief when he stepped down from the saddle. He ordered his men to check their carbines, then he studied the camp below.

Mackenzie's battle report said the camp "was situated on the North Fork of the Red River about seven miles as nearly as can be judged above the mouth of McClellan Creek." Some 262 lodges made the camp the largest of several scattered along the two streams. That meant at least 500 warriors, more than two-to-one odds against the troopers. A vast herd of 3,000 horses and mules grazed some distance from the camp. "Light cavalry," whatever its quality and quantity, didn't function so well afoot. And Sergeant Wilson could see squaws drying meat for the winter, a sure sign of an opportunity for tactical surprise.

About 4 p.m. — three hours after the first sighting of the mule tracks — the Colonel formed the five troops into a compact column. Then he ordered the charge and led off at a gallop. Down the slope thundered 242 horses. The Comanches had been safe here so long they hadn't taken any precautions against a surprise attack. This enabled the soldiers to almost reach the village before they were discovered, although it is hard to imagine that many soldiers going unnoticed while galloping more than three miles.

Wilson knew they had been spotted when he saw the Indian boys guarding the herd stampede the mounts toward the camp. D Troop veered off to intercept the herd.

"Right front into lines," Mackenzie hand signaled. The

column swung around into lines abreast at the edge of the camp. Indians scrambled about everywhere.

Whoops and ragged gunfire broke out as the yellowlegs came within range. A, F and L Troops charged on into the main part of the camp, while I Troop fought around the edge, driving warriors before them toward the river. The sharp bank of the stream afforded some protection for the Comanches, but I Troop simply rode over them. Surviving Indians fled upstream.

The first horses to jump down to the river bed mired in the quicksand. Wilson managed to keep his mount out of the trap and reined in a moment while other horses tried to fight their way clear. They only floundered. One of the trapped riders was Lieutenant Hudson, I Troop commander. Colonel Mackenzie saw his plight and shouted above the gunfire and horse screams, "Sergeant Wilson, take command of the troop and charge. Hold the right village until ordered out."

Wilson nodded his understanding and motioned for those whose mounts could move to follow him. Then he spurred after the fleeing Indians. The pursuit took the remnants of the troop to a smaller camp somewhat detached from the main village. Here Wilson dismounted his men. Every fourth man became a horseholder, while the others stalked through the camp firing at warriors foolish enough to stand against them.

Wilson's revolver grew hot in his hand as he fired at any movement. The bark of rifles and carbines and the lighter crack of revolvers sounded sharp against cries from both sides. The assorted smells of an Indian camp and the biting stench of gunpowder made breathing difficult. But Wilson led the steady march on through the village. Most of the warriors fell back. The others died. The troop occupied the camp until sunset, then rejoined the main command.

Four troopers died and several suffered wounds in the battle. The bodies of 23 warriors were found. At least that many more were believed to have fallen in a deep pool of water behind the embankment where the Comanches staged their main resistance. Captives included 130 women, children and old men, several of them wounded, and 3,000 horses and mules.

The troopers burned all the lodges, the winter supply of meat, robes and all the clothing except what the prisoners wore or carried. Nothing was left that would be of value to the escaped warriors.

Sometime after dark the command marched two miles and dry camped among some sandhills. That night the fugitive warriors swooped down on the camp and stampeded the captured animals. In later campaigns, Mackenzie would shoot all captured mounts to avoid a repetition of this.

During the long trip home, seven of the prisoners died from wounds. I Troop took the rest to Fort Concho for the winter. The remaining warriors — who had escaped at the cost of losing their families and means of existence — surrendered the following spring at the Fort Sill Reservation. Their families joined them there soon afterward.

For taking command of the troop and routing the smaller village, Wilson received his second Medal of Honor. Two of his men and five from other troops participating in the battle also received the medal.

The following year, Wilson accompanied Mackenzie on his famous invasion of Mexico to destroy the home base of marauding Indians who were making raids across the border. In 1874, word reached the Fourth Cavalry at Fort Sill that Comanche Chief Mowri wanted to bring his band to the reservation. At Mackenzie's request, Wilson located the band in the staked plains and explained the terms under which they might come to the reservation. It took him four days to convince them to surrender.

After the Custer "massacre" in 1876, the Fourth Cavalry was ordered to Camp Robinson, Nebraska, to help run down the Sioux and Cheyenne. Wilson scouted for one of the expeditions.

Available records show little else about Wilson until 1890. Still in the Army after 25 years, he helped organize the Medal of Honor Legion and was elected first Inspector General of the organization.

Wilson was never well known outside his own regiment. Today, he is just another unknown soldier who followed the guidon across the frontier.

CHAPTER SEVEN

Albert Weisbogel
(1844-?)

The smallest of all the double winners of the Medal of Honor at four feet, eleven inches, Albert Weisbogel of New Orleans began his first enlistment as an ordinary seaman 13 January 1869, in New York. A dark-haired, skinny little bruiser, he followed a career somewhat typical of the bluejackets of that era.

Most of this three-and-a-half-year enlistment he served in European waters on two steam sloops of war protecting American shipping vessels in an age when there was little danger of their being molested. The cruise, then, was much of what Navy recruiters have been promising for two centuries — seeing the world.

Following his first enlistment after only a month as a civilian, Al re-enlisted as a captain of the mizzen top (sails on the mast nearest the stern of a ship). He shipped out on the **USS Benecia,** a sloop-of-war, in the North Pacific Squadron protecting American shipping in Mexican, Central American and Hawaiian waters. The cruise was another one of those that Navy recruiters boasted about. The ports of call were not as sophisticated as European ports, but the duty and the weather were mostly pleasant.

Al often caught the attention of his shipmates who liked to watch his tiny figure in the rigging overhead. He showed greater ease there than many of them exhibited on the solid deck. Regardless of how the seas were running, he was totally fearless anywhere aloft.

Turbulent weather sometimes interrupted the relaxed routine of the cruise. A sudden storm 11 January 1874, in the Hawaiian area slashed at the squadron for hours. The 250-foot **Benecia** with her 2400-ton displacement rode the waves fairly well, but at one point a giant wave swept a crewman overboard. The chances of a swimmer surviving in that kind of turbulence were slight, but the diminutive Al leaped into the sea to help his shipmate.

At first Al wasn't even certain he could fight his way through to the other crewman, or even survive himself. Fortunately, the water was warm. Al managed to reach the half-dead crewman who could no longer keep his head above water.

Al tried to tell the man to relax. Nearly twice Al's size, the seaman was too far gone to resist. Al turned him on his back and treaded water as best he could in such massive waves and swells. He was just about played out when the lifeline came down from the ship.

For this act of courage, Al received his first Medal of Honor.

The **Benecia** sailed into Pearl Harbor in November 1874, picked up the new, pro-American King Kalakaua and his attendants, then sailed 29 November for San Francisco. The towering king took a quick liking to the daring little mite. Al spent many hours with the king, and hated to see him debark in San Francisco.

A ten-week cruise to Alaska completed Al's second enlistment.

This time Al lasted six weeks in civilian life before the sea called him back. He re-enlisted 2 November 1875, in New York, again as a captain of the mizzen top. He served his third three-year cruise aboard the **USS Plymouth**, a

1122-ton, wooden-hulled screw top sloop-of-war operating along the Atlantic coast and in the Caribbean. A storm in the latter provided him with another opportunity for a medal 27 April 1876.

The **Plymouth** climbed high on the giant swells, then dropped into troughs with a battering force. When Al heard the dreaded cry of "man overboard," he quickly spotted the man and saw his ineffective swimming efforts. So, he plunged into the sea to help him.

Screams from the drowning crewman spurred Al in his greatest swimming effort, but it still took precious minutes to reach the man. By that time the man appeared only half conscious, choking on the sea water in his lungs. He weighed well over 200 pounds but Al towed him with one arm, while fighting the sea with the other for a quarter-hour before a lifeline reached them from the lurching **Plymouth.**

For this rescue effort, Al received his second Medal of Honor. His enlistment expired in September 1875.

Six weeks later, Al signed up for another three years, this time as captain of the top (sails). He spent most of the hitch aboard the **USS Adams**, a wooden screw gunboat patrolling in the Pacific. Back in civilian life again, he lasted an entire three months.

Al's final enlistment ran from 15 July 1882, to 23 December 1885, another adventure-filled period of his service. The entire cruise was spent on a voyage around the world through the straits of Gibralter and the Suez Canal down to Bombay, around to China and across the Pacific back to New York. It was the cruise every sailor dreams of but few ever make.

Al retired after 16 years service, almost all of it at sea, 23 December 1885, at New York.

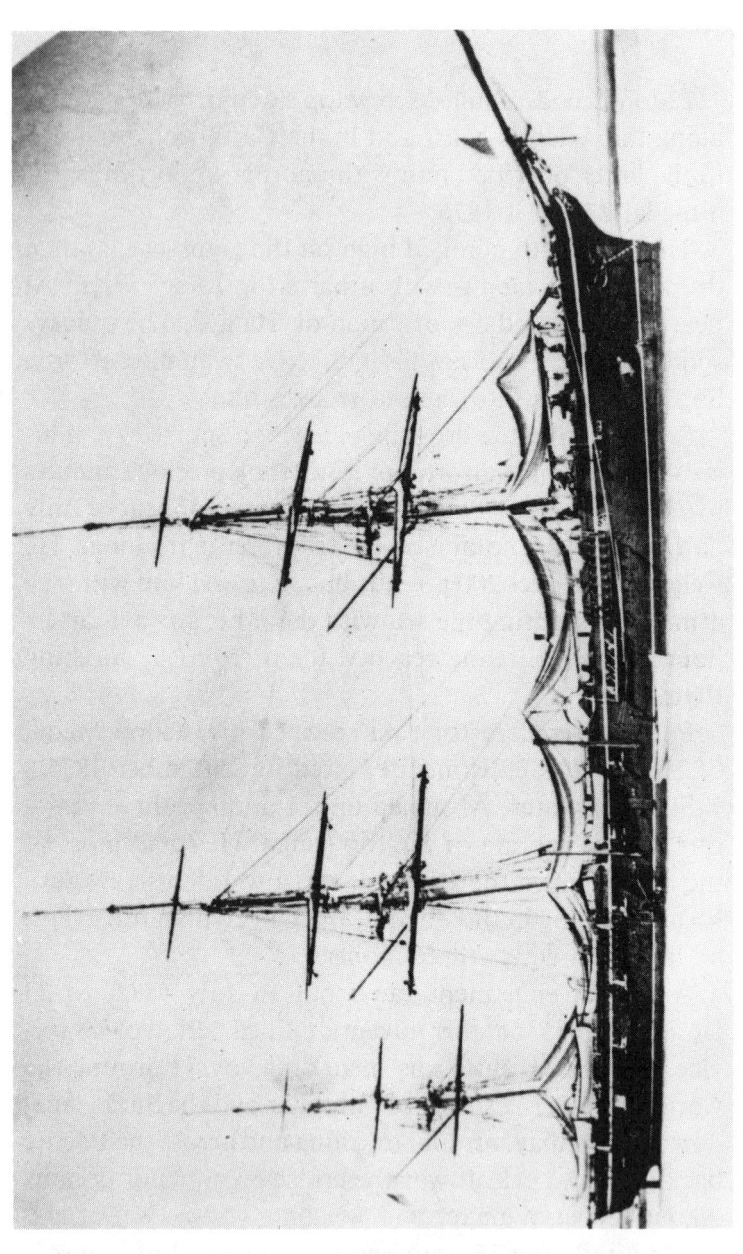

SEVENTH DOUBLE WINNER Albert Weisbogel served aboard this ship, the USS BENICIA, when he earned his first Medal of Honor in 1876.

CHAPTER EIGHT

Henry Hogan
(?-?)

Another Irish emigrant, Henry Hogan, was the last of the old army Indian fighters to earn two Medals of Honor. His 15 years service in the army spanned the Civil War and numerous battles in the Indian Wars of the west that followed.

Though as cool and dependable as William Wilson or Patrick Leonard, Hogan lacked Wilson's dash and Leonard's almost reckless love for a fight. He didn't mind a good scrap, but his courage was more the steady, tenacious type — somewhat like that of Frank Baldwin. His first sergeant's stripes showed his worth in the eyes of his commanding officer, the incomparable Colonel Nelson A. Miles, himself a Medal of Honor winner.

During his thirteenth year of service, Hogan was first sergeant of Company G, 5th U.S. Infantry, at Fort Leavenworth, Kansas. Less than a month after Custer's death on the Little Bighorn, the Fifth Infantry joined the swarm of soldiers scouring the northwest for Sioux and Cheyenne responsible for the stunning defeat. But the gigantic force had split and scattered, easily evading the bluecoats.

In early September, the Fifth Infantry built a cantonment where the Tongue River emptied into the

Yellowstone River. Its mission was to patrol the Yellowstone looking for hostile bands crossing the stream. A large band of Sioux led by Sitting Bull did cross early in October. Colonel Miles pursued with 394 foot soldiers, including Hogan. This was the beginning of a long winter campaign against the Sioux.

The first snow of winter held back just long enough for the Fifth Infantry to overtake the fugitives in the early afternoon of 20 October. As G Company marched at the head of the column along Cedar Creek, Hogan studied the cottonwoods at the water's edge. He had that edgy feeling a professional soldier sometimes gets when he suspects the presence of an unseen enemy.

The column passed the trees without incident, so Hogan studied the next cover — bluffs not far ahead. Suddenly and soundlessly at least 1,000 warriors appeared along the bluffs, rifles ready. The Colonel saw the hostiles at the same time and deployed the men in battle lines, hardly slowing the foward movement. Various historians speculate that this steady but unhurried march forward impressed Sitting Bull. Others think the old chief was just tired of fighting and wanted to rest up for the winter. Whatever his reason, he sent a rider with a flag of truce to meet the oncoming soldiers. The Colonel halted the regiment long enough to learn from the rider that Sitting Bull wanted a conference with Bearcoat (Miles, who was famous for his winter coat made of bearskin).

The name Sitting Bull passed through the command in moments, making some of the recruits a little nervous and some of the old timers a little eager. Even Hogan wondered how many of the warriors on those bluffs carried weapons stripped from the bodies of Custer's men. But he stared sharply along the ranks of his men to quell the chatter before too many of them got the jitters.

While the soldiers watched from the south side and the

Indians from the north, the chiefs, officers and interpreters met about mid-way between the lines. Colonel Miles wanted the Indians to surrender and go to a reservation. Sitting Bull wanted the soldiers to withdraw. Hogan couldn't hear any of this, but the violent gestures of the two made the impasse clear enough.

The parley ended abruptly without any agreement, except to talk again the next day. The Fifth withdrew three miles and camped in some timber along a creek. A fourth of the men stood guard at all times, but few of the others did much sleeping. The specter of the Little Bighorn four months earlier was strong.

At daylight the regiment marched back toward the parley site, and again the officers and chiefs met between the lines, with the same lack of results. But this time Miles ended the talks with an ultimatum — surrender in fifteen minutes or fight. The Colonel returned to his troops and deployed them in battle lines. At the end of fifteen minutes, he ordered the lines forward. Rifle fire shattered the stillness.

The Indians set fire to the prairie grass, but the soldiers marched on through the sporadic flames and sniping. Breathing became difficult, but the volume of shooting increased. The Indians fell back from their positions before the steady pressure. As always in battle, the examples of a few kept the others from faltering.

Sometimes Hogan barked orders to those showing reluctance to keep up, but mostly he just set an example by staying a little ahead of his men and disregarding the shots kicking up dirt near him. Carefully he selected his targets and fired unhurriedly. His courage filtered down to the less hardy men.

Seven miles from the parley site the soldiers drove the Sioux out of their own camp and continued the slow, steady march. Warriors now surrounded the smaller force, but the soldiers formed a hollow square and maintained a blistering fire that withered each attack.

Cavalry could have tried to overrun the hostiles, but infantry could only press on at a slow pace through the dwindling light of day. They camped soon after dark in a valley surrounded by bluffs and hills. They slept little.

At first light they marched, again under ragged fire from a few of the hostiles. Soon even these few galloped on down the valley. For the rest of the day the infantry trudged on without opposition, and without extra speed. Another night camp and half-day's march — now 43 miles from the site of the battle — brought them to the Yellowstone River, where most of the Sioux had already forded and the rest were crossing. As the soldiers swung around into battle lines, a rider came toward them with a white flag. Miles halted the regiment.

All the main chiefs except Sitting Bull came back across the river to talk. This time they agreed to surrender and gave up their weapons and five chiefs as hostages to insure their 2,000 people would go to the Agency instead of disappearing into the night. Sitting Bull continued his flight, but with only a fragment of his people

The regiment returned to the cantonment 3 November after a 300-mile march. After resting two days, the same five companies took to the field again.

Hogan and five of his men were among 31 awarded Medals of Honor for courage displayed during the battle. No single acts of valor were cited, just "gallantry in action" for the examples they set in continually pressing forward under heavy fire against nearly three-to-one odds. Actually, this was only one of three battles cited in the decorations. All 31 repeated their performances — inspiring others with disregard for personal safety — against the Sioux 18 December at Redwater Creek, Montana, and in the Wolf Mountains, Montana battle with Crazy Horse

8 January 1877. (Author's note: These two battles are described in the chapter on Frank Baldwin.)

The winter campaign eventually forced most of the hostiles to reservations. Only Sitting Bull and a minority of his once great nation remained at large. They fled to Canada. This should have brought peace to the northern plains, but it didn't.

Far west of Sioux country, the Nez Perce Indians — peaceful throughout their history but now robbed of their tribal lands in Oregon and Idaho, and otherwise mistreated by greedy settlers — exploded in a running war the Army couldn't handle. Chief Joseph now wanted peace and believed he would find it only in Canada with Sitting Bull. Reluctantly, he led his people, perhaps 800 of them counting non-combatants, on a 2,000-mile fighting retreat southeast, then back northeast into Montana.

The Army dogged the Nez Perce all the way. Each time the soldiers caught up, the Indians cut them to pieces, then continued their flight.

Finally only the forces of Colonel Miles on the Yellowstone appeared to have any chance of intercepting the fugitives. Accordingly, a mixed force of scouts, mounted infantry and cavalry — totaling 350 men and including Hogan's Company G — left the cantonment at the mouth of the Tongue 18 September 1877. They rode northwest, dragging two artillery pieces.

Neither Hogan nor his men handled their mounts with much skill, but they kept up with the cavalry in spite of raw bottoms. Six days later the column reached the Missouri River. They couldn't ford the Big Muddy, but a river boat happened along and ferried them across.

Hard riding until 29 September brought the force within sight of the Bear Paw Mountains in Montana. Deep in the mountains, 50 miles away, smoke drifted up from the fires of a large camp about 30 miles from Canada. The Nez Perce were only a day's march from refuge.

Hogan could sense an excitement in his men now. What a prize for a small force, if it could do what 5,000 other soldiers could not. The First Sergeant grinned a little, causing some of his men to josh him a bit. He ignored the banter.

The column moved on at a fast trot, hardly pausing all day. Soon after they camped for the night, rains soaked them and continued almost to first light. No one did much sleeping. They rode on early, and soon found a wide trail of trampled grass. They galloped for eight miles, until the scouts reported the Nez Perce camp was over the next ridge.

Colonel Miles halted the column to prepare for battle. Hogan rode along the line of his men, making sure each one checked his carbine. Up ahead the Indian scouts stripped off their clothes and painted their faces.

The cavalry galloped on first, about 8 a.m., while the mounted infantry tried to get untangled from the pack mules. Hogan heard the sharp chatter of rifles as the cavalry reached the hostile camp somewhere up ahead, to the north. He reached the ridgetop in time to see the cavalry already in retreat before a devastating fire. In the valley below, he saw smoke puffs and muzzle flashes in ravines near a creek and on bluffs along both sides of the narrow valley. Squaws and children fled the village, running from the sounds of battle.

On order, the infantry came "left front into line," dismounted and took prone positions along the ridge. The nearest hostiles fired from ditches about 200 yards down the slope. Hogan shot one Indian crouching behind a bush, then knocked sand into the face of another in a ditch.

For several minutes the heavy fire filled the valley. Then

Hogan's G Company and two other companies charged, shooting and shouting. But the Nez Perce marksmanship thinned their ranks quickly. The soldiers faltered. Some withdrew. Lieutenant Henry Romeyn, G Company commander, charged on with Hogan and a few others. Not 20 yards from the Indians the Lieutenant staggered, then plunged to the ground. This broke up the charge. Hogan called to three of his men, motioned them to follow, and ran on toward the Lieutenant. Every Indian rifle seemed to snarl at him, but he ignored the fury and ran on. When he reached the Lieutenant, he shielded him with his body while checking to see if he was still alive. Blood spurted from a hole in the Lieutenant's right lung and from several lesser wounds, but he still breathed. In fact, he recognized Hogan.

"Get out of here, Sergeant. I'm finished."

"We'll get you back, sir."

The Indians couldn't miss at that range. But they did. Maybe they wanted to miss. Old west Indians believed the highest honor a man could achieve was by rescuing a comrade at great personal risk. Any fool could kill. That didn't take courage. Perhaps they spared Hogan because of this.

At any rate, Hogan's men reached them without wounds. The four of them then grabbed the arms and legs of the Lieutenant and ran back up the slope with slugs tearing up dirt all around them. And every man escaped unharmed.

Romeyn not only survived that day and received the Medal of Honor for leading the charge, but he personally recommended Hogan for his second Medal of Honor. Hogan was the last Army man to get a second award.

At the moment, however, Hogan was busy taking command of the company. Nearly 400 soldiers surrounded the Indian camp now, outnumbering the Nez Perce combatants about four-to-one. There was no escape, but word came down the line that an Indian rider had broken through and was headed toward Sitting Bull in Canada, just 30 miles away. That gave the soldiers some uneasy thoughts as the hours of the siege dragged on into the night.

Snow and bitter cold hit them soon after dark. Hogan kept half his men on the line and sent the others for firewood. They couldn't find any. The barren country offered them nothing but more snow and slashing winds. Tents provided some protection for the wounded; the rest just toughed it out through the long and sleepless night.

At dawn snow covered the area. Hogan shivered through another frozen day and night of sporadic firing, warmed only by the arrival of one artillery piece during the night. The cannon did most of the firing on the third and fourth days, eventually forcing the Indians to surrender on the morning of 4 October, five days after the first charge. Chief Joseph came out of the Indian position under a flag of truce, followed slowly by his warriors who surrendered their weapons as they reached the soldiers. Only 87 Nez Perce fighting men remained of the 300 who had begun fighting the whites several months earlier at the beginning of the longest running battle in history. About 250 squaws and children surrendered also. In the siege just completed, the Indians had 17 dead and 40 wounded, the soldiers 24 dead and 42 wounded.

When Colonel Miles ordered food and blankets for the frozen and starving Nez Perce, the soldiers cheered. The after-battle warm feeling each side felt for the other made the whole affair seem a little absurd. Hogan never forgot the compassion he felt for the gallant Nez Perce.

Hogan's second Medal of Honor made him only the eighth double winner, a mighty elite group. But little attention was accorded him then or later. He retired from the Army in 1879, after 15 years service, and settled down in Miles City, Montana, a lusty frontier settlement named for his former commanding officer, Colonel Miles.

CHAPTER NINE

Robert Sweeney
(1853-?)

The only Negro among the double winners of the Medal of Honor was Ordinary Seaman Robert Sweeney, a native of Monseral, West Indies, who enlisted for a three-year hitch 17 September 1881, in Philadelphia. Twenty-eight years of age, he stood five feet, ten inches tall.

Sweeney served his first two years aboard the **USS Kearsage**, a 201-foot screw sloop of 1,550 tons. The 20-year-old ship patrolled the Atlantic from Newfoundland to the Caribbean and the east coast of Panama.

The month following Sweeney's enlistment, the **Kearsage** sailed into historic Hampton Roads, Virginia, a wide, bay-like channel through which the waters of the James, Nansemond and Elizabeth Rivers flow into Chesapeake Bay. Nineteen years earlier the ironclads **Monitor** and **Merrimac** had fought their famous battle there. For most of America's history it has been a major rendezvous for the U.S. Navy.

The **Kearsage** entered the channel 26 October 1881, in the middle of a storm and a "strongly running ride." A crewman fell overboard screaming he couldn't swim. Sweeney plunged in after him only to find the tide nearly too much for any swimmer. It nearly sucked him under several times before he reached the floundering sailor.

Sweeney fought the nearly overwhelming tide another 20 minutes before the **Kearsage** could reach him and his burden.

For risking his life to save another, Sweeney received his first Medal of Honor.

Sweeney found his remaining 23 months aboard the **Kearsage** uneventful, a regular routine of standing watches, relaxing on the fantail, enjoying the greatness of the sea and feeling the insignificance of man in the middle of it.

For his final year of service he was transferred 6 September 1883, to the **USS Yantic**, which patrolled the Atlantic from Maine to the West Indies and eastward to the coast of Europe. This was the golden era for bluejackets on American ships, sailing on fascinating voyages followed by long periods in foreign ports. Ships still used a combination of sails and steam engines, and seamanship was the prized skill of the fleet.

Three months after boarding the **Yantic**, Sweeney's second great moment arrived. The ship left the Atlantic heading toward the New York Navy Yard just ahead of a storm. The veteran crew, old hands at sudden Caribbean storms, didn't even get excited about this one. But the heavy fog did give them the jitters. As they steamed in near to where the U.S. Navy Base was supposed to be, they passed close to the **USS Jamestown**. In a momentary easing of the fog, Sweeney saw a crewman of the **Jamestown** fall overboard. The fog hid the man immediately as he yelled for help.

Sweeney leaped over the side into the swirling waters. Once there, he wasn't certain he had done the wise thing for he couldn't see anything at sea level. The terror of the unknown would have discouraged most, but Sweeney swam toward the now screaming man. When Sweeney reached him, the stricken man fought him briefly until

Sweeney could calm his terror.

Then a new problem presented itself. Where were the ships? Sweeney's normally excellent sense of direction failed him here. He tread water, holding up the man, straining to hear something that would help. Only the sound of the waves broke the silence. He shouted. No answer.

Then a foghorn sounded from one of the ships, guiding him in his feeble efforts against the powerful swells. He still didn't see the ship until he nearly bumped into the starboard side. Then he heard shouts from the deck about the same time the life lines came down to him.

For this second rescue, Sweeney received his second Medal of Honor.

Sweeney completed his hitch eight months later and received an honorable discharge. This single tour was his only naval service. He, too, vanished into the obscurity that shrouds most of the double winners.

Official U. S. Navy Photograph

NINTH DOUBLE WINNER Robert Sweeney served aboard this ship, the USS KEARSAGE, when he earned his first medal.

NINTH DOUBLE WINNER Robert Sweeney served aboard this ship, the USS JAMESTOWN, when he earned his second Medal of Honor in 1883.

ANOTHER VIEW of the USS JAMESTOWN, ship of Robert Sweeney when he earned his second Medal of Honor in 1883. This photo was made about 1889 at the Portsmouth Navy Yard, New Hampshire. The ship just aft of the JAMESTOWN is the USS CONSTITUTION, used as a receiving ship at the time of this photo.

Naval History Photograph

A THIRD VIEW of the USS JAMESTOWN about 1890.

CHAPTER TEN

Louis Williams (1845-86)

The third double winner of the Medal of Honor to serve under a name other than that he was born with was Ludwig Andreas Olsen, born in 1845, in Christiana, Norway. He went to sea as a teenager, about 1862. He changed his name to Louis Williams in 1868, taking the place of a sailor by that name who had deserted from a British merchant ship in San Francisco Bay. He used the name for the rest of his life.

After ten years, mostly at sea (1862-72), Williams found himself back in San Francisco. He began a series of enlistments in the U.S. Navy spanning 14 years, patrolling the Pacific and the coast of South America. His records list him as five feet, eight inches tall, with gray eyes, light hair and florid complexion.

Williams' first cruise ended in Japan where he was discharged two years later but re-enlisted the following year for China service. His third hitch began 12 August 1878, aboard the **USS Lackawanna** protecting American shipping interests in the Pacific.

The ship eventually returned to San Francisco, where Williams signed up for his fourth hitch 18 October 1880, as a captain of the top. For a year he helped refit the sloop **USS Jamestown** in San Francisco Bay. Then he went back aboard the **Lackawanna** for the remaining four years and four months of his life.

The **Lackawanna** was a fairly common screw sloop of that period, built back in the early part of the Civil War and now an elderly 20 years old. She served well patrolling the Pacific.

The months slipped by peacefully, other than encounters with storms and seas. The **Lackawanna** sailed to Hawaii 16 March 1883.

Since the Hawaiian Islands were first discovered, sailors have found them — particularly Oahu — a choice liberty port. As the ship neared the island, Landsman Tomas Moran found the sight of Oahu and the memory of its pleasures too much to resist. He decided to desert. Over the side he went, but he didn't count on the gigantic surf for which the island is famous. Scarcely 150 yards from the ship he found himself drowning. He screamed for help.

Williams heard the cry of his shipmate and plunged overboard. His swim through that surf became something of a legend of that era. He couldn't locate Moran at first, and the powerful current nearly overpowered him. At one point he nearly gave up the search, but then Moran popped up on the crest of a roaring swell. Williams finally fought his way to the unconscious man. By now the ship had come about and approached the pair. Lifelines brought them aboard. Williams suffered severe strain to various organs of his body from the effort.

A Medal of Honor was presented Williams for his heroism.

He re-enlisted 26 October 1883, remaining aboard the **Lackawanna,** patrolling the Pacific. On 13 June 1884, the ship cruised along the coastal waters near Callao, Peru. A tropical storm swept a friend of Williams — William Cruise — into the boiling sea.

Once again Williams jumped overboard. Only those who have known the terror of raging seas can appreciate the courage it took for Williams to risk his life a second time to rescue a shipmate. He struggled to his drowning friend and brought him back to the ship. For this gallantry, Williams received his second Medal of Honor.

Williams died 20 February 1886, in the U.S. Naval Hospital, Brooklyn, from complications caused by the severe strain to his body during the two rescues. He was buried in Cypress Hills National Cemetery near John Cooper.

U.S. Naval Historic Center Photograph

***TENTH DOUBLE WINNER** Louis Williams served this ship, the USS LACKAWANA, when he earned both of his medals.*

CHAPTER ELEVEN

Daniel Joseph Daly
(1873-1937)

Picking the mightiest of all Marines would be extremely difficult, considering the number of legends the Corps has produced. But two commandants of the Marine Corps claimed a half-pint Irish newsboy from the asphalt jungle of New York City could outfight them all. Certainly Daniel Joseph Daly became the most famous Marine Corps legend, twice awarded the Medal of Honor and recommended for a third. With jutting chin and flint eyes, he stood five-feet, six inches and 130 pounds of rompin', stompin' destruction.

Born 11 November 1873, in Glen Cove, Long Island, Daly learned to scrap by whipping rival newsboys for the best sales corners of New York. With this training behind him, at the age of 12 he became a semi-pro boxer in sports clubs, when he was not selling papers.

Daily enlisted in the Marines 10 January 1899. After boot training he served with the Asiatic Fleet aboard the light Cruiser **USS Newark.** The Boxer Rebellion brought the **Newark** to the coast of China in May 1900. Daly knew little about what was going on in China, except that American legation personnel faced slaughter ashore.

The events that brought the Americans to the shore of

China had begun long before, as six great powers — Russia, Germany, Britain, France, Italy, and Japan — divided China into "spheres of influence," treating their individual spheres almost like colonies. Russian aggression in Manchuria, and German and French seizures of Chinese port cities further angered the already sullen but impotent Chinese.

Two years of drought caused millions of Chinese to starve. This catastrophe also was blamed on the foreign devils. Foreign missionaries converted thousands of native Chinese to the Christian faith, angering Buddhist priests who fanned the hatred of the foreigners.

Still, China lacked the unity and military might to drive out the foreigners. So, a secret society of terrorists became active in 1898, killing foreigners in general, and Christian missionaries and their converts in particular. The society called itself the "I Ho Chuan" (Fists of Righteous Harmony). The rest of the world called them the "Boxers." Mostly ignorant peasants from the rural areas, the Boxers soon spread into every village and city, murdering and torturing even their own people who opposed them. Their slogan, "exterminate the foreigners," drew millions into their ranks. Decades of real and imagined wrongs poured forth in a blood bath for China. How many Chinese Christians died will never be known, but about 250 missionaries lost their heads. By early 1900, the Empress of China began to encourage the Boxers, hoping they might actually succeed in driving the foreigners into the sea. The Imperial Army left the Boxers alone, and by May 1900, they even rampaged through the streets of the capital city, Peking.

Though the United States was not involved in the exploitation of China, it provided some of the missionaries and a small legation in Peking, along with ten other nations. With the Boxers surrounding the foreign compound screaming "Sha, Sha" (Kill! Kill!), the various legations called for help. This call brought the **Newark** 12 miles offshore 29 May 1900, to the Taku sand bar which blocked a closer approach by large ships.

From the bow of the **Newark**, Daly could see 16 other warships flying the flags of 7 nations — an international fleet soon to land an international relief force. He could make out the flags of England, France, Germany, Japan, Italy and Russia, the six colonial powers.

At dawn the scrawny little private scrambled down a net into a landing craft alongside the ship. He was one of 48 Marines and 3 sailors representing the United States in the joint venture. From other ships, Marines of six nations packed into assorted small craft for the same purpose.

The American boat shoved off from the **Newark**, moving slowly toward the coast. American Marines of that era, particularly those of the Asiatic Fleet, were a rugged lot who paid scant attention to a greenhorn runt like Daly. The coming weeks would launch the greatest legend of the legendary leathernecks, but likely Daly's only thoughts at the time concerned the coming fight. He might even have had the untried soldier's usual first-combat doubts, but that seems unlikely. He'd been fighting for 14 of his 26 years, in one way or another.

Some of the Marines grumbled about the water spraying over the bow of the boat. Daly maintained his characteristic silence. He squinted from under his campaign hat at the giant cannons poking out of concrete and steel emplacements, protecting the mouth of the Pei-Ho (North) River against invaders from the sea. The big guns seemed to point directly at the American barge. If they opened up, the matchbox craft would vanish. But the guns remained silent. The Empress was not yet ready for open war with the combined powers of the world.

The boat passed under the guns and turned up the river, pulling in at a small village where the Marines and sailors landed on the muddy bank. They marched to the nearby railroad and boarded boxcars behind an ancient Chinese locomotive. Somehow the old engine pulled the cars 30 miles to Tientsin, a city of more than one million.

Two days later, a six-nation relief force of 337 officers and men seized another antique Chinese train and chugged inland toward the capital city, Peking, 80 miles distant. The train arrived at the end of its track, about four miles from the walled city, after dark. A column formed, with the Americans in front.

"Fix bayonets," ordered Captain Myers, commanding the Americans. Cold steel clicked into place.

"Forward, MARCH."

The Yanks stepped out smartly, confident of their ability to cope with what lay ahead. The Lee rifle with bayonet attached was nearly as long as Daly, but that didn't bother him. He knew how to use it.

The column reached the walled city about 8 p.m. and marched through a pagoda-topped gate into the city. Daly's first glimpse of Peking told him what the coming weeks would be like. Thousands of torches revealed sullen Chinese faces lining the street. Not a sound came from them, but Daly could feel the hatred. And the smell of China — open sewers, rotting garbage and unwashed bodies — would stay with him forever. The Yanks went through another gate with a pagoda atop it, then marched into the foreign compound as 500 trapped residents of the legations shouted wildly. The bearded American minister, Edwin Conger, reached the Yanks first.

"Thank God you have come," Conger blurted out. "Now we are safe."

As Conger finished, Daly heard an uproar on the far side of the 40-foot wall. He glanced up as a wave of long spears hurtled over the wall. Spear heads clanked against the cobblestones, throwing out sparks. *Some safety.*

But the spear throwing appeared to be the dying gasp of the mob. Within minutes, the streets were deserted and quiet. The unorganized mob, despite its great superiority in numbers, wanted no part of the professional soldiers armed with rifles and automatic weapons.

The first part of June remained fairly peaceful in the legation area, except for an occasional sniper's bullet. But the threat of an impending explosion lay heavy everywhere. Daly could smell it, feel it, taste it. Reports from outside the compound only confirmed what he already knew. A batch of 40 Belgian railroad workers ran into an ambush enroute to Tientsin, losing 7 men 2 June. The next day, 40 miles south of the city, 2 British missionaries lost their heads. However, that afternoon nearly a hundred German and Austrian sailors arrived from the coast unmolested. The Boxers still feared the foreign uniform.

Missionaries and their converts swarmed into the compound from all the surrounding area with new reports of murders. Feeding them became a problem. A larger relief force from the coast would be here soon, Daly heard; but they didn't arrive 11 June as scheduled. The mobs outside the legation became more threatening after that, and the Americans looked around the compound for ways of defending it. Daly followed Captain Myers on a tour of the small area, 4,000 feet wide and the same distance long. The Tartar wall, 40 feet high and 40 feet wide, protected the south side of the compound, but Imperial soldiers occupied the top of the wall. Ramps on the east and west side of the compound led up to the top of the wall. The section of wall between them would have to be cleared of Chinese if shooting started.

The Imperial City wall, also 40 feet high and 40 feet

wide, but pink in color and topped with yellow tiles, protected most of the west and half the north side of the quarter. Daly could see the top of the royal palace just inside the Imperial City wall. No direct trouble would come from there. Return fire might hit the old Empress.

The weak side of the foreign compound lay to the east, bounded only by a 200-foot wide street. Nearly every day, one or more snipers on rooftops across the street fired into the compound. Any defense line on that side would have to be erected inside the compound area.

The quarter contained the legation buildings of 11 nations — the United States, England, France, Germany, Austria-Hungary, Holland, Belgium, Italy, Japan, Russia and Spain. A shallow sewage canal ran north and south near enough to the middle of the area for its pungent odor to reach all the legation compound. Some 2,000 Chinese Christian converts crowded into the small area, seeking protection from the fanatics.

Boxers cut the last remaining telegraph line 13 June. The defenders would have no word of the relief column until it arrived — if it did. In the afternoon Daly heard screaming and shouting on the east side of the quarter. He followed other Marines on the double, in time to see hundreds of Chinese peasants spill through a gate in the Tartar wall, shouting, "Sha, Sha" (Kill, Kill) and slashing Chinese young and old with knives and crude farming tools. The Marines formed a line but the Boxers stayed on the far side of the wide street, smashing their way through shops and homes. Each wore a scarlet band around his head or waist. The mob seemed totally without reason, driving their own people before them in terror. Smoke and flames from burning buildings soon filled the sky. The horde moved on north, its line of progress marked by more smoke and flames.

In the following days the Boxer bands continued their

reign of terror through the city, often killing, burning and looting, near the compound. Imperial soldiers on the Tartar wall watched without interference as the rampage grew in fury. Flames engulfed a nearby fireworks shop 19 July, bringing a series of explosions, an omen of things to come. That afternoon the Imperial government ordered all foreigners out of China. This amounted to a declaration of war against the 11 powers.

The German minister left the compound the next morning to protest the edict. He traveled only a short distance before a Boxer shot him dead. Daly rushed out with a party to rescue the body, but thousands of screaming Boxers drove them back into the legation area with spears and rifles. That afternoon a hidden sniper shot down a French Marine.

The final phase of the siege of Peking was underway, with the Imperial Army joining the Boxers, making 50,000 Chinese against 400 armed defenders. The Empress was finished with pretense.

The first step for the defenders was to take over that portion of the Tartar wall overlooking the compound. Imperial soldiers manned the section and from their position could make the compound indefensible. The area between the two ramps leading down into the compound would have to be secured immediately. German Marines charged up the eastern ramp, the one nearest their legation, while the American Marines battled up the western ramp near their legation. Apparently the Chinese soldiers had not expected this attack because the Marines of both nations reached the top of the wall without serious opposition. But once there, resistance stiffened.

Daly emptied his rifle, then went to work with rifle butt and bayonet. In minutes, the German and American Marines met, with no enemy left between them. They turned back-to-back and charged the remaining Chinese within rifle shot of the legations. This was Daly's first real combat, and no one ever again held light regard for his fighting prowess. He proved himself the best of the Marines.

The Germans formed a line on the east end of the wall section to be held, and the Americans did the same on the west end. During the day they drove back several counterattacks with accurate rifle fire. Meanwhile, Chinese Christians from the legation area brought up sandbags for barricades. The Boxers and Imperial soldiers erected brick barricades not far from the American position, building the brick wall high enough to permit them to fire down behind the American barrier. Only darkness saved the Americans from immediate slaughter.

That night Captain Myers, commanding the American Marines, called for reinforcements from the German and British Marines, and for a few Russian sailors. Daly hunkered down on the Captain's right side, listening to the soft spoken instructions. They would attack about 2 a.m., when the Chinese would least expect it. They would charge single file down each side of the 40-foot wall, because when the Chinese heard them coming, likely they would fire down the middle.

At the appointed time, the Marines removed sandbags from each end of their barrier. Then 2 files of 25 men each moved out, quietly at first. Daly watched the dim form just ahead of him to avoid bumping into the man in the dark. He shuffled about 25 yards before he heard firing from the Chinese position. The slugs came down the middle, as the Captain had anticipated. The attackers charged around the ends of the Chinese barricade, driving the Imperial troops and Boxers back. Daly bayoneted one soldier through the middle and smashed the face of another with his rifle butt. In seconds they were beyond the barrier and among the makeshift tents and shacks.

They kicked in the flimsy structures and bayoneted the Chinese before many of them could shake loose from the debris. In a few vicious minutes, 50 Marines drove hundreds of Chinese fleeing along the top of the wall.

For the next two days the Marines stayed behind their own sandbags, firing only at some careless Chinese soldiers 100 yards farther west on the wall. They now held the section of the wall where the legation was near enough to be fired on by rifles.

Daly seldom left the wall during the entire seige. The position, while dangerous, afforded the best view of both the compound and the city. He watched the legation guards below establish barricades of upturned carts and sandbags made from every possible color of silk curtains, dresses, bedspreads and other finery.

On the south side of the wall the streets below soon filled with the bloated bodies of Chinese. The blistering heat putrified the flesh quickly. The stench, added to the normal rotten smell of China, sickened Daly at first. And, as the Boxers burned more and more buildings in the area, often with bodies inside, Daly found it more difficult to breathe without nausea. He would never forget that smell, though war would be his way of life for two decades.

About 500 soldiers, 500 civilian foreigners and more than 2,000 Christian Chinese crowded into the compound. To feed the 3,000 mouths soon became a major problem. About 155 horses provided them with fresh meat, but even the horses became scarce in the latter weeks of the siege.

A relief column from the coast should arrive any day, the ministers kept saying. Most everyone seemed to believe it, but Daly had his doubts.

Eight days of constant and vicious attacks by 20,000 Imperial soldiers and 30,000 Boxers began 24 June. Daly didn't leave the wall once during that period, and slept seldom. On the first of the eight days the Marines charged west 90 yards, driving the Chinese back to a burnt-out pagoda over a gate in the wall. About a hundred yards from the pagoda the Marines dropped behind a barricade and fired briefly at the tower. They they pulled a dirty Yankee trick.

They brought up a 400-rounds-per-minute Colt machine gun and set it up in position, hiding it from view of those in the tower. Then most of the Marines faked a retreat back along the wall. As expected, the Chinese burst forth from the pagoda in hot pursuit, shouting in triumph. The hidden Marines allowed the chargers to come within 20 yards of the sandbags before they opened fire with the giant Colt, literally ripping the attackers apart. The "retreating" Marines hurried back to help finish the job and found few targets left for their rifles. This site became their permanent position for the rest of the siege, though they did have to give it up briefly the next day.

On the morning of 25 June, more and more Boxers crowded onto the wall on the far side of the pagoda, obviously massing for an attack. These were anxious hours for the small group of Yanks. But the blackest moment came about noon when the Chinese set up a cannon in the tower. Blasts from the field piece smashed into the barricade, slowly knocking it apart. Daly knew when to keep down. One glance at the cannon was enough for him. Within half an hour the Marines had to abandon what was left of the position.

From their former position a thousand yards east of the pagoda, the Marines rested three hours while Captain Myers went to the compound and arranged for coolies to help rebuild the advance position if the Americans could recapture it. With this arrangement completed, he returned to the wall and led the Marines in another charge to the remains of the barricade a hundred yards from the tower. They caught the Chinese by surprise and reached the position without serious injury. They couldn't move around without drawing cannon fire from the tower. However, they didn't have to move.

About 4 p.m., Daily heard a weird, reverberating sound — a giant horn blowing — from Imperial City. From every direction, horns, bugles and various other sound contraptions answered almost in unison. All enemy firing ceased. The reason for the cease fire will never be known, but the Marines made good use of the time by rebuilding the barricade across the 40-foot width of the wall.

Firing resumed at 8 p.m. The barricade held; but with the Chinese firing up to 200,000 rounds of all sizes every 24-hour period, the casualties mounted among the defenders. Heat prostration and dysentery claimed others. Daly figured he had a pretty good idea of what hell was like.

About dark 27 June, something new confronted the Marines. Some 200 Boxers charged their position, forced on by the bayonets of Imperial soldiers. Apparently it was getting more difficult for the Imperial Army to recruit "true believers" who thought their faith made them bullet proof. Daly emptied his rifle before the front ranks reached the barricade. Then he jumped the barricade with others, thrusting and slashing with his bayonet, and hammering with his rifle butt. He knocked two Boxers over the side of the wall. Only half the original force retreated. The others lay dead on the wall or on the street 40 feet below.

The long days of heat, dust and gunpowder, with no bathing or even a change of clothes, left the Marines a scroungy looking bunch. Their own body smell soon rivaled that of the rotting dead below. And Daly didn't think he could stand another bite of horse meat and rice.

One break in the monotony came when an enemy cannon shell ignited a fire in one of the compound buildings. The ladies of the legations formed a bucket brigade to fight the flames, using chamber pots for buckets. One of the few stories the reticent Daly ever related later was this one; he always admired the plucky females and their chamber-pot brigade.

Rumors about a relief column spread, then died out, only to begin again. But the column didn't come. And the firing seldom ceased. Once Daly awoke from a brief nap in a dead stillness, a brief one; he had grown so accustomed to the shooting the lack of it awakened him. Another time he looked up at a buddy just as a sniper's bullet ripped through the friend's head, splattering blood and brains on Daly. The sight should have sickened him, but he was now toughened beyond such reaction. However, this toughness helped make him an incredible fighter.

The long drought, blamed by the Boxers on the foreign devils, ended 30 June in a rainstorm so heavy that Daly couldn't see more than a few feet down the wall. The Marines danced along the top of the wall like kids, oblivious to the possibility of snipers. Daly covered his rifle with the remains of a silk sandbag, turned his face skyward, and clamped his eyes shut against the deluge.

The rain brought some new worries. As the flimsy sandbags soaked up water, they split apart. They would have to be replaced that night. And a wet countryside would slow the relief column, if there was one. More than ever, Daly had his doubts about that.

The dry and blistering heat of the previous weeks now turned to steaming, broiling heat 1 July. Daly preferred the former, even with the dust. And the stench of rotting flesh remained. About 9 a.m., heavy gunfire broke out at the German barricade to the east. Daly didn't pay much attention until he heard a Marine cursing. Glancing around, he saw the entire German force retreating down the east ramp, leaving their barricade unmanned. That left the American Marines in a crossfire. Captain Myers ordered an immediate withdrawal down the west ramp. An hour later the American forces returned to their barricade, as the Chinese had not occupied it. The Germans returned to their wall but never did recapture their former position.

The reason for the Chinese failure to occupy the American position likely was their preoccupation with building a tower near the burnt-out pagoda. By late the next day (2 July), Chinese atop the tower could almost fire down on the Marines behind their barricade. The Marines would have to capture the tower that night, or retreat along the wall. Captain Myers commanded the attack force, including some British and Russian Marines, totaling 56 men. The attack was set for 3 a.m.

Daly slept in the early part of the evening, unmoved by what lay ahead. Rain awoke him sometime after midnight and he huddled up against the sandbags, protecting his rifle.

A couple of hours later, Captain Myers quietly assembled all the force in a tight group. He spoke so softly Daly could barely hear him, though he was less than dozen feet away; nor could he see all the men in the blackness of the night. The captain warned of the danger ahead — that he had advised against the attack, but had been overruled by the legation heads — orders were orders — the attack must be made, even to the death of every man — if they failed others would have to die in another attempt — surprise was essential, so no noise until the first contact was made — anyone who didn't want to go could pull out. He stopped then, waiting.

"Captain," someone said from the back of the group.

"I got a sore arm and wouldn't be much use to you."

Captain Myers said nothing, nor did anyone else. The man mumbled something else, then trotted back along the wall toward the ramp. Daly dropped his chin in disbelief, as the rain grew heavier. Idly he wondered if a man charging in the dark might run right off the wall to the cobblestones 40 feet below.

Softly the Captain passed the word to move out. Daly led the force over the barricade, walking humped over and with his bayonet thrust well ahead. The older hands willingly allowed the "little bundle of destruction" the point position. He scrambled over the first Chinese barricade and gutted a surprised soldier before he heard his first sound — a thin cry from his left. In the darkness he could see only a few feet, but he slashed, smashed and stabbed at Chinese soldiers and Boxers alike. Not a shot was fired.

Without pausing, the force charged on to the tower that threatened their own position. Again, surprise favored the attackers; but this time shooting broke loose, ending the struggle swiftly. The Chinese fled, leaving about 30 dead behind. Two American Marines lay dead also, and Captain Myers lay in a pool of his own blood, flowing from a severe spear wound in his leg.

The legation defenders, long low on ammunition, captured an abundance of rifles and ammo in the raid — enough to keep them going for the rest of the seige. Without it, and without the destruction of the tower, the compound likely would not have held out until relief finally did arrive.

For those on the wall, the next couple of weeks were the most restful, with only occasional sniping from the demoralized Chinese. But the stench continued to bite at their nostrils. Some of the Marines vomited occasionally when the smell was the worst. The compound smelled almost as bad as the rest of the city, because sanitation there was impossible. The flies and mosquitoes seemed as big and mean as hawks, with a million-to-one ratio over the "foreign devils."

Casualties grew and the food supply decreased, and still the tiny legation guard withstood the cream of the Imperial Army as well as the fanatical Boxers. Attacks continued all around the perimeter, except against the American position on the west end of the wall. The Chinese there had learned their lesson and never again tried more than sporadic sniping.

The citation for Daly's first Medal of Honor says only that on "14 August 1900, Daly distinguished himself by meritorious conduct." But the citation actually covered several heroic acts during the 56-day seige. His greatest deed of valor came late in the afternoon of 13 July when Boxers and soldiers once again drove the German Marines back from their position on the east end of the wall. At dusk the American Marines relieved the Germans at the makeshift barricade to which they had retreated. With a quick glance, Captain Hall, the new CO of the Americans, could see that the position would have to be strengthened if it was to be held. Rebuilding it would take most of the night. He told Daly he needed a volunteer to creep out front and hold back the Chinese while the repairs were made.

"I'm your man," Daly replied.

The Captain and Daly scrambled over what barricade already existed and trotted quietly through the darkness. The city south of the wall blazed in one giant inferno, lighting up the south side of the top wall. The north side remained dark. About 100 yards out, Daly heard Chinese voices from behind a line of rubble thrown across the top of the wall. Light from the burning city glinted on rifles, spears and swords protruding above the top of the

40-foot-long barricade. Daly followed the Captain into a bastion in the side of the north wall. Here they squatted and listened to the voices, a meaningless jabber except for occasional laughter.

"I won't order you to stay out here," the Captain said softly. "But if you can hold them back tonight, they'll never drive us back tomorrow."

"I'll stay," the little rookie whispered back. "See you tomorrow."

The Captain nodded, reluctantly. From all accounts, Daly probably thought no more of the job than any other that might have needed doing. Captain Hall handed him some extra bandoliers of ammunition, squeezed his arm, and vanished into the night.

Daly squatted just inside the bastion, with a pile of ammunition in front of him ready for use. A few minutes dragged by silently, then two Boxers started over the rubble. Daly squeezed off two quick shots and the heads vanished. All chatter ceased on the far side of the position. Daly expected a rush, since the rifle shots obviously were so close. But none came. Instead, small bunches tried to sneak over various sections of the barricade. Firelight showed their heads clearly each time, and Daly put a bullet into each one.

Well into the night four Boxers leaped over the top of the barricade simultaneously, before Daly could sight their heads. All four charged him, waving huge swords and shouting the familiar "Sha, Sha." He stopped the first one with a single shot in the heart, and worked the bolt action on his Lee rifle rapidly three times, hitting each of the other three Boxers. But the small bore weapon lacked the striking power to stop the fanatics. Daly jumped to his feet and shot the nearest charger a second time, knocking him into oblivion below the wall. There was no time to work the bolt action again, so he thrust his bayonet into the chest of the third man. As he pulled the steel free, he whirled around to avoid a sword swung at him, and used the same motion to drive his rifle butt into the jaw of the final Boxer, knocking him off the wall.

Daly jumped back into the bastion, as many rifles opened fire at him from the Chinese breastwork. Spears and arrows filled the air also. But the Chinese couldn't see him on the dark side of the wall.

Still the Chinese didn't get the message. Any mass attack would have overpowered Daly, armed only with the bolt action rifle. But all night long they continued coming in small batches. Six came once, and died within as many seconds from one shot each.

According to legend, dawn found 200 Chinese dead from Daly's one-man war. Likely this figure is exaggerated — but not by much.

Captain Hall greeted Daly as he scrambled over the now sturdy American barricade at dawn. "A great job," Hall praised. "You bought us the time we needed."

Daly shrugged it off and headed for his bedroll and sleep. The old timers of the outfit marvelled at the slight form sleeping there. They had just witnessed the beginning of a legend, and they knew it.

Heavy firing continued through the day, and Daly was up at noon for another round. Some of the Marines made such a fuss over his recent accomplishment that he had to give them a good cussing.

An uneasy truce began 16 July, with no serious attacks for the next two weeks. A couple of nighttime raids caused only a slight stir. Others figured this meant the relief force must be near. Daly gave it little thought.

Early in August, the legations butchered the last of their racing ponies, and began digging up roots of plants and trees for food. For ammunition the legation troops crept out at night to capture bandoliers from dead Boxers and Imperial soldiers.

The first word from the outside world in nearly two months reached the compound 10 August, a message carried from the relief force by a Chinese Christian. The note said the force would arrive 13 or 14 August. What was left of the legation forces broke into wild cheers. The taciturn Daly joined them.

But the seige wasn't over yet. Two days later an underground mine exploded under a building housing children and nuns. More than 100 Chinese women and babies were killed.

Another explosion knocked out an eight-foot section of the eastern perimeter line 13 August, but the Boxers failed to follow through with a charge.

The relief column arrived the next day.

Following the Boxer Rebellion, Daly served aboard half a dozen ships in the Pacific and Caribbean area, fought in some of the "banana wars" south of the border, and trained recruits in the States. With the years, also, came the rank of gunnery sergeant and the reputation as a Marine's Marine. His erect military appearance offset his lack of size. Though a strict disciplinarian, he treated his men fairly, earning their admiration and respect. His old boxing skills served him well also, and he became known as one of the Corps' best brawlers. He never sought that kind of trouble, but neither did he back away from it. His small stature occasionally fooled some bully into mistaking him for a soft touch.

Though he shunned recognition, Daly couldn't dodge all the accord due him. The public had just about forgotten his Peking heroics when he shipped out on the cruiser **USS Springfield** early in 1911. One night he went topside in time to spot a gasoline fire spreading toward a powder magazine. In seconds the entire ship could have been blown apart and 500 men killed. But Daly fought the flames away from the magazine, saving the ship and suffering severe burns that put him in sick bay for several weeks. To make him even more uncomfortable, he received a written commendation from the Secretary of the Navy and an oral commendation from the commandant of the Marine Corps who visited him there. By the time this recognition died down, Daly earned another medal at Vera Cruz, Mexico, but circumstances prevented him from receiving it.

The United States refused to recognize the dictatorship set up in 1913, in Mexico by General Huerta, who took over the government by a treacherous coup and was unable to establish a stable government during his entire 17-month reign. Internal strife, threatening the lives and property of Americans, plus several border and port city incidents — mostly trivial — caused President Woodrow Wilson to send warships to the harbors at Tampico and Vera Cruz.

When Wilson learned a shipload of German machine guns and ammunition was enroute to Vera Cruz, he feared the weapons might be used in a war against the United States. He wanted the Huerta government overthrown anyway. So, he ordered American Naval and Marine forces already in Vera Cruz harbor to land and seize the customs house to prevent receipt of the weapons.

American ships in the harbor included the battleships **Florida** and **Utah,** and the auxiliary cruiser **Prairie.**

The landing force debarked in motor launches and whaleboats towed by launches at mid-morning, on an intensely hot and sultry day. Heavy swells rocked the craft as the First Marine Regiment — 600 officers and men — and the First Seaman Regiment — also 600 strong — headed ashore. Both regiments carried bolt action Springfield '03 rifles. The Marines wore khaki fatigues with broad-brimmed campaign hats, leggings and knapsack rolls. Some of the sailors wore undress blues and some undress whites, all with leggings, haversacks and waist belts of ammunition.

Among the Marines in one motor launch, the now legendary Daly sat quietly, much as he had 14 years earlier when he went ashore in China for his first combat. There was even an old fort guarding the harbor, as there had been in China. But this time it posed no threat. A faded sign on the scabby looking structure proclaimed it to be a prison now. Whitewash peeled off its walls.

Ahead, each building of the city seemed to be painted a different color, standing out against the green covered, low sand hills in the background. The tallest building reared up only three stories high, despite the fact this was the main seaport of Mexico. Church bells sounded somewhere in the city, reminding Daly this was Sunday morning.

Daly's launch reached the huge pier about 11:20 a.m. He led his platoon up the granite steps, glancing only briefly at the line of curious civilians along the seawall. A small cluster of American civilians waving the stars and stripes cheered the Marines. Only then did the Mexican civilians seem to understand this was a hostile landing force. They scattered. So did the hundreds of black vultures along the seawall.

The Marines fanned out from the waterfront area, and Daly could hear the clatter of shops closing along the streets. He led his men across a grassy plaza as a stillness settled on the city. Dead animals and garbage lay everywhere, rotting in the searing heat.

Within 25 minutes the Marines occupied the railroad terminal, the terminal hotel, cable house and other buildings without opposition. Then a Navy signalman climbed atop a hotel roof to send a message to the admiral on the **Florida**. A single rifle shot toppled him to the cobblestone street below.

The battle began.

Daly kept his men under cover until the order came to fan out and set up positions to block the western approaches to the Terminal Yard. A ragged line of rifle fire broke loose from roof tops nearest the Marine positions, from about 100 snipers. Daly directed return fire from his platoon. Some of the snipers wore uniforms, some the white cotton of peons, and some prison garb. The Americans learned later the Mexicans had emptied the old fortress of its prisoners to help fight the Yankees.

The German ship bringing arms to the Mexican government reached port about 1:30 p.m. the first day, when firing was hotter than the scorching weather. A naval party from the U.S. flagship took a launch to the German vessel and boarded her. They told the German skipper the customs house was under American control and warned him against attempting to unload his cargo or leave the port. The prudent captain decided that was good advice. He quickly dropped anchor. In fact, he didn't even send a boat ashore to check the validity of the Yankee claim.

The multi-colored lower class homes and businesses nearest the waterfront were cleaned out first, then the brick and stone quality homes more distant from the stench and filth. The Mexican troops were disposed of the first day and half the city was occupied. But irregular forces and convicts maintained a strong resistance at scattered points and in the outskirts of the city.

During the night, additional American warships arrived with reinforcements. The brass in Washington now realized the entire city would have to be cleaned out and cabled the order to Mexico. Two battalions of Marines and a naval battalion landed early the second morning. This brought 2,000 Marines and 1,000 seamen ashore.

During the morning of the second day, a group of

snipers pinned down Daly's platoon in an arroyo. The thick adobe walls shielded the Mexicans completely. Every time one of the platoon tried to move he drew heavy fire from the windows.

Finally Daly lost his patience.

He told his men to stay put and crawled off along the arroyo for a short distance. He left the ditch and crawled through sand mounds to the backside of the house, then charged the back door. The snipers apparently hadn't expected trouble from that direction, for they had left the door unguarded.

Daly shouldered through the back door and found seven startled Mexicans inside. He shot five of them before they could fire at him. Then he killed the other two with his bayonet. He stepped out the front door, blood still showing on his bayonet, and motioned his men on.

Not even a letter of commendation was accorded Daly for this bit of bravery, but it didn't bother him any. He wouldn't even talk about the incident to others.

Organized resistance ended the second day with the occupation of the entire city, but some sniping continued for several days. The U.S. had 17 dead and 63 wounded. An estimated 230 Mexicans died and about that many suffered wounds.

The following 15 July, Huerta resigned the presidency, but his successor displeased President Wilson equally as much.

The Daly legend grew some more in 1915, when the U.S. seamen and Marines landed in Haiti. For decades the black republic had known only unstable and corrupt government accompanied by revolution and assassinations. The head of the government usually was the man backed by the Cacos, thousands of bandits who had named themselves after the red-plumed bird of prey that lived off weaker birds.

Early governments had borrowed heavily from European countries, and incoming regimes were unable to pay off the debts. Creditor nations threatened to send military forces to the tiny Caribbean country. To ward off such intervention in violation of the Monroe Doctrine, to protect American lives in Haiti, and to restore order in place of chaos, United States bluejackets and Marines occupied the country from 1915 to 1934.

Among the first Marines to land in the capital city, Port-au-Prince, in 1915, was the reticent, pugnacious Daly. The first act of the Marines was to disarm and disband the native army which was made up of little more than bandits. The Marines, with bayonets ready, stood in the aisles while the national assembly elected a new president — one free of the domination of the Cacos who kept the country in turmoil.

Port-au-Prince became peaceful enough, but the rest of the country remained under Caco control. Stable government would never exist nationally until their power was broken. Accordingly, Marines set up outposts in key areas in the north, where the bandits were strongest. The regiment of Daly went to Cap Haiten on the northern coast, not far from the Dominican Republic border to the east.

Scattered skirmishes followed, but no real progress toward stability developed. Two-thirds of the country was rugged, mountainous terrain. Travel was difficult. Hiding was easy, but the Marines eventually learned that the Cacos operated out of three strongholds hidden somewhere in a mountainous area. Their stronghold covered an area 20 by 60 miles, not counting the hills. A two-pronged campaign was planned. A recon patrol would find the strongholds, then a larger force would destroy them.

The regimental colonel decided 3,000 Marines would

be needed to sweep the area and locate the strongholds. Major Smedley Butler, typically, volunteered to accomplish the job with 26 Marines, with the stipulation that he be allowed to choose his own men. The colonel called his bluff.

Butler picked old hands seasoned in battle in China, the Philippines and various Latin republics. For his top sergeant he picked the toughest of the lot, hard-boiled Dan Daly — despite the sergeant's age, 41, and his iron gray hair now turning white.

For once the Marines rode horses and led pack mules. Up and down 100 miles of treacherous mountain trails the 27 Marines rode for 2 days and nights without sleep, and without contact with Cacos. On the third weary morning, while riding single file along a trail, they encountered a gigantic Negro standing in a clearing. Butler nicknamed him Apeman because his long arms dangled to his knees. Cacos normally wore patches of red on the arm or chest, denoting the red plume of the Caco bird. Apeman wore no such badge so he didn't get shot.

Butler ordered a brief rest while he offered Apeman $5 to lead them to the Caco strongholds, or a bullet if he refused. Apeman agreed. Unknown to the Marines, the giant was a Caco sent to lead them into a trap. Daly and Butler were not naive enough to trust the big brute, but they figured they would find their quarry either way.

Apeman led them across a chill stream and up a mountain, along faint, winding trails. About 3 p.m., they found a Caco stronghold — Fort Capois — about a mile ahead and clinging to a cone-shaped mountain peak a thousand feet above them. Hundreds of blacks wearing red patches on arms and breasts moved around an elaborate system of trenches and stone walls encircling the peak.

"Twenty-seven of us will never take that, Major," Daly said.

"We're not supposed to," Butler answered. "Just find it and report back."

Both felt the itch to fight, but neither was foolish enough to think they should. They withdrew.

For several hours the small detachment rode over a network of mountain trails, until finally no one but Apeman knew where they were. It began to rain, slowing movement and obscuring vision. Apeman walked ahead of the patrol, with Butler just behind. Daly rode last, keeping the others from straggling. His suspicions about the guide grew stronger.

As the dim light of day faded, the rain grew colder. Most men Daly's age would have wondered why they were not back in the States, sitting in front of a warm fire. But this was Daly's life. He coveted no other, though the rain dampened his ardor some.

After dark the patrol halted at the edge of a sheer canyon wall. Daly could hear rushing water at least 200 feet below. The trail down into the canyon followed a ledge maybe 30 inches wide, and Daly could see only 3 or 4 feet ahead. No telling what the trail would be like farther down. It would be like descending into the bowels of the earth. But Apeman insisted this was the only way back to the coast.

Daly ordered his men to tie white handkerchiefs around their necks for identification purposes, in case of attack. The smell of trouble lay everywhere like damp smoke. Daly and Butler decided they should lead their mounts, with each man holding the tail of the horse in front of him. Butler led off down the steep trail into the blackness.

The roar of the river grew louder with each step, and no one hurried down. The teamwork was what might be expected of veteran Marines. Daly didn't have to kick any tails to keep them moving.

When he reached the bottom of the canyon, Butler kept

on going into the river, still leading his horse. When he and his orderly reached the far side, shouting broke out behind them. Someone had lost his hold on the tail of the horse in front of him. Butler handed the orderly a flashlight to mark the way. This light brought a fusilade of shots from the bushes on both sides of the Marines, the closest about 100 yards away. Apeman had led them into a trap.

The Marines flattened out on the ground, and the shots passed over them. From the rifle flashes, Daly figured there were about 400 Cacos. He sent the rest of his men on into the river, until the last one passed, then he followed. He saw no point in firing blindly, and the Cacos couldn't tell exactly where they were in the blackness. All 27 Marines crossed without a casualty, but the 12 pack mules all died from bullets, taking their supplies and the machine gun to the bottom of the river.

The Marines crawled up from the river, holding reins in their left hands. Daly was tempted to leave his animal behind, but he resisted the thought. About a mile up the slope from the river the Marines set up a position in a dished out area. Then Butler sought Daly.

"Set up the machine gun here, Dan."

"Sorry, Major. We lost it in the river."

The stunning impact of the statement kept Butler silent for a moment. They would just have to do their best without it, Butler mumbled. He moved off in the darkness.

Daly said nothing to anyone. He just dumped his gear, except for a knife, and crawled back down the trail to the river. Legend, fiction and fact about the next few hours are so mixed up no one will ever know all the truth. The laconic Daly told precious little of it himself. According to various accounts, he killed from one to seven Cacos with his knife on the way to the river.

Once there, Daly plunged into the rushing current and began searching for the dead mules. Several times he came up for air. Finally, he found the machine gun and slashed the straps holding it to the pack animal. How he carried the heavy weapon ashore while fighting the pull of the river is hard to imagine. At some point, the blackness of the night softened just enough for several Cacos to spot him in the river. They began shooting at him, but he continued to dive for the 30 caliber ammunition cans. This took three trips to the shore with snipers blasting away at him.

According to one account, Daly screamed as if mortally wounded, swam underwater to some underbrush and hid out until the Cacos thought him dead. Another version claims he killed three Cacos on the shore when he brought up a can of ammo. Only Daly knew for sure and he never told. Both stories could be true.

Daly crawled out of the river, strapped the gun on his back and picked up the ammo cans. Under the 200-pound load, the 130-pound bulldog staggered the long mile back to the Marine position, reaching there an hour after leaving. In the dark he took the machine gun apart, cleaned it, reassembled it, and set it up for firing. Then he searched out Butler.

"The machine gun is ready for firing, Major."

For once the talkative Butler couldn't find a thing to say. He just shook his head and grinned. Daly received his second Medal of Honor for this effort, at Butler's recommendation.

Several times that night the Marines moved to new positions, just moments before the Cacos attacked the spot where they had been. Daly could hear the bandits thrashing about, screaming insults and chopping away at the underbrush. When they got too close, he scattered them by hosing down the area with 30 caliber bullets. They blew shrill sounds on shell horns and shouted that they would cut the Marines to pieces.

Just before dawn 22 October 1915, the Marines set up their final position. There would be no more hiding now — just jaw to jaw battle. But the Cacos withdrew to a small fort about 400 yards away, Fort Dipitie, smallest of the three strongholds. They had had enough of the machine gun.

The 27 Marines then attacked the fort held by nearly 400 Cacos, drove them out and hunted down many of those who fled. The Marines killed 75 Cacos without losing a man. Only one Marine suffered a minor wound. They destroyed the fort and huts, then returned to base.

A few days later, three companies of Marines and two companies of sailors captured Fort Capois after a brief skirmish without casualties on either side. A detachment of Marines remained there to prevent the Cacos from filtering back.

The Marines captured the third and final stronghold a short time later, ending insurrection in Haiti for several years.

Daly managed to get duty in France during World War I, despite his 45 years and now white hair. He wrote a blazing final chapter to his military career with heroic feats that sound more like fiction than fact.

The Germany Army broke through the French line 28 May 1918, at Chemin des Dames and by 4 June drove to a point within 40 miles of Paris. Loss of the city might have meant an overall German victory. Almost certainly it would have knocked the French out of the war. The deepest penetration of the offense, and the war, was a forested area known as Belleau Wood. Here the drive stalled against the American Fifth and Sixth Marines.

Daly's regiment moved into the line at the southern end of the Wood 1 June. The "little legend" commanded the

73rd machine gun company of the Sixth Marines. He dug in his men and guns near the village of Lucy-le-Bocages, at the southwest corner of Belleau Wood. The dense forest, a mile and a half long north to south, and a half mile wide, hid whatever was inside it. Three times 2 June, the Germans attacked the Marine position, but artillery, machine guns and Marine rifles drove them back with heavy losses.

In the afternoon and evening of 5 June, the Germans fired 2,000 artillery shells in the section around Daly. Soon after dark one shell started a fire in a nearby ammunition dump. Flames, exploding shells and tracer bullets made the place look like a Fourth of July celebration. Daly rounded up "volunteers" from his company and ran into the inferno. Within minutes they snuffed out the flames, preventing the entire dump from exploding.

Another legend about Daly resulted from the activity the next day, 6 June, when the regiment attacked Belleau Wood. The French reported the wood lightly held by the Germans, when actually it was almost a solid machine gun nest. Some 1,200 Germans with 200 machine guns holed up in gullies and behind huge boulders, among trees often too close together to penetrate except along narrow paths.

In position for the assault set for 5 p.m., Daly didn't like the open field of green wheat his men would have to cross before reaching the edge of the forest 400 yards away. But he'd see to it they charged according to plan. A pre-assault barrage started pounding the area at 4:30 p.m. Trees shattered under the blasts, exposing the ruggedness of the terrain, but no Germans.

The signal to charge came at 5 p.m. The Marines moved out in straight lines, according to orders based on the foolish advice of the "more experienced" French high command. A massive concentration of German machine guns slashed at the ranks. When the younger men wavered in their charge, seeking cover, Daly waved his rifle over his head and shouted, "Come on you sons-of-bitches. Do you want to live forever?"

The Marines charged with new vigor. But even Daly's iron will couldn't achieve the impossible. The German machine guns ripped the lines apart. Survivors dropped to the ground, with only wheat to protect them. They were pinned down until dark, then what was left of them crawled back to their starting point. But they would be back, using Indian-style tactics.

The following day the Germans bombarded the sector so long that many of Daly's green recruits began to get nervous. To calm them, he left the protection of the trenches and walked in the open from one gun emplacement to another, totally ignoring the barrage, encouraging and cheering up his men.

A German heavy machine gun sneaked in close to Daly's position 10 June and opened fire. Daly reacted completely in character, grabbing some grenades and charging. Near the gun he dived into a ditch long enough to toss three grenades, silencing the weapon. Then he drew his 45-caliber pistol and continued his charge. He shot the officer commanding the gun crew, then swung his pistol on the 14 enlisted men still alive. They promptly surrendered.

Later in the day, a battle raged for control of the village of Bouresches near the southeast corner of Belleau Wood. Several times Daly ran out between the lines to rescue wounded men.

For his actions of 5-7 and 10 June, Daly was recommended for a third Medal of Honor. But higher military authority didn't think anyone should have three, so he received the second highest decoration, the Navy Cross and the Distinguished Service Cross, and, from the

French, the Medaille Militaire. General Pershing also offered him a battlefield commission, but he rejected it.

Daly suffered a shell fragment wound in his leg 21 June but still crawled out between the lines three times to drag in wounded men. He wanted to go again but was ordered to the field hospital. Medics there found him more than they could handle and released him for duty just to get rid of him.

The battle for Belleau Wood ended 26 June, the first offensive victory for the Americans, at the frightful price of 8,000 casualties.

Daly later led an attack in the Meuse-Argonne assault, near the end of the war, receiving a bullet wound in the shoulder and a shrapnel wound in his leg. For him, that ended the war and his fighting career.

Completing his 20 years service in 1919, he retired from active duty, more to get away from newspaper publicity than anything else. For the next 17 years, he lived quietly with his sister in New York and worked as a bank guard.

Daly died of a heart attack in 1937, at the age of 63, and was buried in Cypress Hills National Cemetery near where he lived. The Navy named a destroyer for him during World War II; otherwise, he remains almost unknown in today's America.

ELEVENTH DOUBLE WINNER Daniel Daly.

CHAPTER TWELVE

John McCloy
(1876-1945)

A superior officer once described John McCloy as "a bull of a man who charged ahead and got things done." That's about the best description that can be offered of the Navy's double winner of the Medal of Honor who became the greatest legend from the enlisted ranks.

Born 30 January 1876, in Brewster, New York, he first enlisted in the Navy 7 March 1898. He served as a seaman aboard the **USS Columbia**, patrolling the Atlantic Coast and Cuba during the Spanish-American War. The ship also landed troops at Guanica, Puerto Rico.

McCloy's first heroic service came one night near Fire Island in the Caribbean, when the **Columbia** collided in the dark with a British steamer. McCloy volunteered for duty in the small boats that fought through the rough seas rescuing survivors of the sinking British ship.

After the war, McCloy went to the Philippines for service on various gunboats during the insurrection there. When the Boxer Rebellion broke out in 1900, he was among those hurried off to China.

Two relief forces from Tientsin attempted to reach Peking during the rebellion. McCloy was in the first one, which left 10 June 1900, ten days before the siege of the legations actually started.

Foreign ministers, worried about the rapid rise in terrorism by Boxers, requested additional guards from the naval vessels of various nations off Taku. Fragments of forces from these ships straggled into Tientsin during the first few days of the month. After some quibbling over who would command, British Admiral Seymore organized an international force of 2,000 men, including 112 American sailors and Marines commanded by naval Captain B. H. McCall.

Admiral Seymore commandeered five trains 10 June 1900, to transport his mixed command and their mountains of equipment 80 miles inland to Peking. The Americans rode an open flatcar of the lead train, unfortunately for them. The train crossed the Pei-Ho River bridge at Yangtsun about noon. One of the Imperial armies camped near the track. The Chinese smiled and waved at the foreign troops, and otherwise seemed friendly enough to McCloy. Now an old salt with the rank of coxswain, he was still young enough to feel the excitement of the adventure.

Not far beyond the city, the lead train grumbled to a halt where the rails had been knocked loose from the ties. The American sailors piled off and began replacing the track. McCloy sweated over the hard labor, listening to the impatient Yanks who claimed they came to fight, not toil in the boiling sun and gagging smell of human waste that fertilized the nearby rice paddies.

The rest of the day followed the same pattern — chug a short distance in a few minutes, then spend many times as long repairing another break in the track. McCloy spent a restless night on the flatcar. The second day was another of short traveling and long stops, with another uncomfortable night stop. The train inched forward for only four miles the third day.

In the afternoon of 13 June, the train halted for more

track repairs near another of the countless mud villages. McCloy helped shove a rail back into place, then heard shouting. He glanced up to see a ragged line of perhaps 200 Boxers — mostly teenagers — charging from the village to the left. Chaos reigned among a big portion of the relief force at this first contact with the enemy, despite the small size of the attackers; but, a few cool heads like McCloy grabbed their rifles and ran to positions well out from the train. McCloy squatted down and raised his rifle, waiting for the Boxers to come into range. Behind him some semblance of a skirmish line began to form, leaving him and a few others as a salient to face the force of the charge.

Some of the Boxers dropped to their knees for brief prayers before continuing the charge. Many carried spears or swords, while others brandished rifles. Ragged firing began down the line of the relief force, but McCloy waited until he had a sure shot. Then he sighted and fired swiftly and mechanically. The charge slowed, but the slaughter continued for 20 minutes before the "invulnerable" Boxers broke into a rout, leaving 60 dead behind.

This was one of four separate actions for which McCloy was cited in his first Medal of Honor decoration. The others would come seven, eight and nine days later.

Resistance from larger forces of Boxers hit the train at later stops during the next few days, as the struggle toward Peking continued by yards instead of miles. The five trains were strung out all the way back to Yangtsun, a point passed the first day by the lead train. Boxers were everywhere, sniping at the train and track workers. Ammunition became scarce an the casualties mounted. In the American force of 112, 3 were killed and 25 wounded. Thirty-two miles from Peking, the trains could move no more. The track simply didn't exist. To go across country, mostly rice paddies, without means of transporting the wounded and equipment, was impossible.

McCloy wasn't in on the council of war among the expedition leaders, but soon learned the results. The trains would return to Yangtsun, where the tracks crossed the Pei Ho River, and proceed to Peking by junks. But getting back to Yangtsun was as difficult as the original trip. Arriving at Yangtsun, they found only four junks which they used simply to cross the river rather than travel up it to Peking. The first relief expedition was rapidly falling apart from lack of ammunition, transport, and growing casualties.

Imperial soldiers now joined the Boxers in the attacks. Even the men in the ranks realized the importance of this. The sound of artillery could be heard from Tientsin, from which they had started 10 June. That could only mean that the city was under siege also, and would be no haven for them even if they could reach it.

The force started back toward Tientsin, nonetheless, marching along the river and using the four junks for equipment and wounded. Each village had to be cleared by heavy fighting — and more casualties. Some of the troops marched along the banks of the river, pulling ropes attached to the junks. McCloy remained out in flanker position, fighting off constant attacks. Half rations and scorching heat left him weak.

A scorching attack by Imperial troops 20 June came close to reaching the strung out international force. Only determined resistance from a small group — including McCloy — broke up the charge. This was the second action for which he was cited. A flesh wound earned him a Purple Heart.

In 3 days of fighting retreat, the force covered only 20 miles, and still had 10 miles to go before reaching the dubious safety of Tientsin. With little food or ammunition left, they trudged another four miles 21 June. After dark, the force spotted some sort of huge structure ahead in the darkness. McCloy could make out the outlines of fort-like walls about 700 feet long. A Chinese voice called out, and somewhere ahead a British officer answered. Hundreds of rifles along the wall opened fire.

McCloy didn't see much of what happened next, but he joined one of the forces storming the walls. From midnight to near dawn the attack continued, then the Chinese fled. In the first light of dawn, the foreigners found themselves in an arsenal they didn't even know existed. It contained 7 million rounds of ammunition for rifles, plus rifles and machine guns, artillery, 15 tons of rice, and an abundance of medical supplies.

As one among those most heroic in capturing the arsenal that night and beating off counterattacks 22 June, McCloy later received the Medal of Honor for services of 13, 20, 21, and 22 June.

The battered force remained in the arsenal six miles from Tientsin until rescued by another relief force 25 June. It returned to Tientsin, too spent to be of further service in the relief of the legations, but having fought well in keeping the road open to Peking.

After Peking, McCloy served on many ships and gunboats, literally sailing the seven seas. From China, he returned to the Philippines for two years fighting against the rebels. He was aboard the gunboat **Gardoqui** when she destroyed insurgent vessels and covered amphibious landings in Manila Bay, Subic Bay, and points in between. When rebels attacked Marines near Bacor, Luzon, McCloy volunteered for the Naval landing team that reinforced the outmanned Marines.

Soon a master of shipboard guns, he impressed his superiors with his performance under fire. He knew many moments of fear, but performed his duties without regard to enemy barrage. When the Army marched north from

Manila toward Olongapo, fire support covering the advance came from the monitor **Monterey**. McCloy was among gunners pinpointing enemy positions along the 60-mile coastal route. At the port of Olongapo, the ship knocked out insurgent guns and defensive positions ahead of the assault. McCloy's appointment as boatswain in 1903, seemed small enough reward.

Later in 1903, McCloy went on reconnaissance missions and helped build signal stations across the route of the Panama Canal. Insects and weather were the chief enemy here. In 1904, Moroccan tribesmen kidnapped some American citizens. McCloy landed with the volunteer force that rescued the Americans.

Cruising the South Atlantic for a couple of years, McCloy hit the usual African and South American ports. In 1905, he cruised the West Indies, then went to France and escorted the body of John Paul Jones to the U.S. Naval Academy at Annapolis. Then he sailed eastward around the world to Japan.

By 1907, McCloy was back in the New York Navy Yard aboard the **USS Hancock.** The **USS Pawnee,** moored alongside, caught fire near magazines loaded with explosives. Spreading to the docks, the flames threatened stores of explosives there also. Among the leaders of the fire fighters saving ship and shore was McCloy.

Other shipboard stations followed for McCloy, bringing him a promotion to chief boatswain. He boarded the **USS Florida** in 1913, cruising the Mediterranean Sea and the West Indies. This put him in position for the landing at Vera Cruz in 1914.

McCloy went into the Vera Cruz battle a chief boatswain with sixteen years service, the epitome of an enlisted sailor, as much a legend in the Navy as Dan Daly was in the Marines. For the landings of 21-22 April 1914, McCloy served as beachmaster, commanding the three motor launches towing the whaleboats of sailors and Marines ashore. Then the launches began hauling in the supplies needed to sustain the fighting, unloading on Pier Four, the main pier of the port.

During the unloading, through the noon hour and past 1 p.m., a steady fire from rifles and small cannons somewhere to the south made the pier hazardous. Several bluejackets fell wounded.

McCloy ordered his boat crews to take cover while he studied the area. The main firing seemed to come from some buildings 200 to 300 yards south of the pier. He spotted Captain Bush assembling a seaman group behind the seawall and dashed over to him.

Could they get some fire support from the ships, McCloy asked?

Captain Bush said he had signaled for help, but the naval gunners couldn't see where the fire was coming from. McCloy said he could take care of that, so the Captain told him to go ahead. The Captain signaled for the **Prairie** to prepare for fire support.

McCloy ran back down the pier to his launches and ordered his crewmen aboard. Each launch carried a one-pound cannon on its bow, fired by a two-man crew. McCloy took the controls of the lead launch. The craft surged into life under full throttle, turning south and running parallel to the beach. The other two launches followed at top speed. When the launches passed across the front of the Naval Academy building, McCloy motioned his gun crews to open fire with their cannon. His one-pounders couldn't penetrate the thick walls, but some found the windows. Mostly, though, he just wanted to draw enemy fire to show the naval gunners where to return fire.

He succeeded.

The Mexicans returned the fire with a wild barrage of

cannon and rifle fire at almost point blank range. They should have blown all three launches out of the water immediately, except their marksmanship wasn't that great.

Completing the first pass, McCloy spun his launch around and back for a second run. The three-inch guns of the **Prairie** opened fire then, pounding into the walls of the academy and piercing the windows.

A small cannon shell hit his steering gear, another penetrated the superstructure somewhat harmlessly, and a third hit a valve on a steam line, stopping the launch dead in the water.

McCloy's engineer patched over the broken valve, enabling the launch to move slowly. McCloy ordered a crewman to take the launch back to Pier Four, then he jumped over to his number two launch and continued the run.

But the Mexican gunners found the second launch, also. The two gun crewmen fell to the deck, one dead, one critical. McCloy felt a rifle slug sear through his right thigh, nearly driving him overboard. But he clenched his teeth, finished the run and came back for a return pass.

Only one of the two buildings — the Naval Academy — still erupted with fire. As McCloy's launches swept by, the **Prairie's** batteries silenced the Academy's fire also. A white flag appeared in one of the windows.

Sailors and Marines ashore, pinned down by the fire from the buildings, cheered lustily and left their cover to continue their missions. McCloy returned to Pier Four and permitted only a brief dressing of his leg wound. Then he spent the next 48 hours working as beachmaster, directing reinforcements on their way, and sending the wounded back to the ships. He left only when the brigade surgeon ordered him to go back to the ship's sick bay.

For his three days service at Vera Cruz, McCloy received his second Medal of Honor, for valor, and his second Purple Heart, for wounds received in action.

After Vera Cruz, McCloy spent several weeks recovering from his thigh wound, then served aboard a pair of battleships. When World War I started, he was commissioned as an ensign, then promoted to lieutenant in 1918. He commanded two auxiliary ships and a mine sweeper during the conflict. He took command of a new minesweeper, the **USS Curlew,** in 1919. For several weeks the **Curlew** "engaged in the difficult and hazardous duty of sweeping for and removing mines of the North Sea Barrage." For this McCloy received the Navy Cross.

Various other sea commands in the Atlantic and Pacific followed for McCloy. He was married in 1927, when 51 years old, and retired the following year with 30 years service. One final bit of recognition was accorded him, in 1942, when the Secretary of the Navy commended him for his various acts of valor and promoted him to lieutenant commander on the retired list. He died 24 May 1945, in Leonia, New Jersey, and was buried in Arlington National Cemetery.

Naval History Photograph

TWELFTH DOUBLE WINNER John McCloy.

CHAPTER THIRTEEN

Smedley D. Butler (1881-1940)

The most colorful and best known of all the double winners of the Medal of Honor was Smedley Darlington Butler. No one who knew him in the beginning of his service would have expected heroic things of him. Even less would they have expected him to become a major general in line for commandant of the Marine Corps. He had received his commission through the political pull of his father, a U.S. congressman, which is seldom any indication of greatness to come.

Born 30 July 1881, in West Chester, Pennsylvania, Butler was reared a Quaker. Something of a rebel during his boyhood, he was sixteen when the Spanish-American War started. He tried to join the Army and the Navy but was too young. Then he threatened to run away from home unless his mother helped him get in the Marines. His congressman father was a close friend of the Marine Corps commandant, and by stretching his age a couple of years, Butler secured a commission as a second lieutenant.

A few weeks later, Butler turned up in Cuba, probably the greenest shavetail in the history of the Corps and a prime candidate for a Spanish bullet. He turned even greener the first time a bullet buzzed over his head. Several times he made an ass of himself trying to act like the Marine officer he wasn't, but the old pros of the Corps liked the punk kid and kept him alive and out of trouble. Like Dan Daly, he was less than average height and never did climb above 130 pounds. Rounded shoulders and a beak nose didn't add anything to his military bearing. But deep set eyes later earned him the nickname of "old gimlet eye."

After the war, Butler went to sea aboard the **USS New York,** still not old enough to shave or act much like a Marine. Then, in April 1899, he shipped out for the Philippines and the insurrection there that would eventually claim more American lives than the war just ended.

Now 18 and a first lieutenant, Butler developed enough leadership to command a company on a patrol out of Cavite, Luzon. He nearly led his men into an ambush on a jungle trail. Premature firing from a trench across the trail sent Butler and his command sprawling to the ground. After a few moments of panic, he led a charge that drove the Filipinos back into some rice paddies. Every insurgent rifle seemed to be aimed just at him, but he plunged on into the waist-deep mud, water and human waste that filled the paddies. The insurgents continued to fall back fighting, finally crossing a river, then breaking into a rout.

Despite the thrill of that first command under fire, Butler still lacked the lust for battle that he developed later. In fact, he was more than just a little scared. But he acquired seasoning in that and other skirmishes, and a touch of the Marine bravado. He still showed signs of immaturity, however, as in his having the Marine Corps emblem tatooed over his entire chest and stomach. The size of the tatoo was intended to outdo smaller ones on his fellow officers. It probably was, and is, an all-time champion.

Butler was in Cavite when word of the Boxer Rebellion reached there. Marines were needed for a second relief force to Peking and Butler volunteered. This would be the campaign that turned him from a boy into a man, but at the time he volunteered he regarded it simply as a grand adventure.

The ship carrying the 100 American Marines reached the Taku sandbar 19 June 1900, the day before the siege started in Peking, and the same day the first relief force crawled slowly back toward Tientsin with the Boxers in pursuit all the way. The Marines commandeered a train and headed for Tientsin, also, but from the coastal side. What could 100 American Marines do to save 1,700 international troops surrounded by 50,000 Chinese in Tientsin? Butler gave it little thought.

The force left at noon, creeping along the battered track in the most ancient train Butler would ever see. In the afternoon, they spotted 400 Russian soldiers marching along the track, and offered them a ride. The heavy built Russians helped in track repairing, probably wondering if the "free" ride was worth it.

Dark found the train 12 miles short of Tientsin, at the former site of a river bridge, blown apart. They abandoned the train early the next morning — 21 June — and marched on, leaving most of their supplies behind.

Butler couldn't tell much about the country they marched through during the next few hours. About dawn he saw a squat, grayish mud village to the south, apparently empty. Just behind the village he could make out the rooftops of Tientsin.

The Russians in front of the column must have been watching the rooftops also, for they walked right into an ambush. At the first crash of rifle fire, Butler sprawled out and crawled over to the edge of the column. Some 6,000 Boxers fired at them from a hidden trench ahead and from the village behind. The heavy fire continued for two hours before the Russians began filtering back, leaving the Marines out front. With three dead and nine wounded, the Marines pulled back also.

With the retreat underway, Butler ordered his sergeant to check the company. The sergeant reported that Private Carter was missing. When last seen, Carter was in a ditch a quarter-mile back. With Lieutenant Harding and four enlisted men, Butler returned to the ambush site, fighting Boxers all the way. Today it would appear ludicrous that 6 Marines could hold 6,000 Chinese fanatics at bay; but it happened then, primarily due to the awe the Chinese felt for foreign soldiers. Most of the Chinese stayed out of rifle range. Those who didn't got shot.

Butler found Carter in the mud hole near the railroad track, groaning in agony from a smashed leg and begging for death. The bone stuck out of his leg. Two of the enlisted men kept the Boxers at a respectable distance with deadly accurate rifle fire, while the other four lifted the wounded man from the ditch and bandaged him as best they could with their shirts. Butler and Harding formed a chair with their hands and arms and picked up Carter. Two of the enlisted men lifted his feet, and in this manner they began the slow job of carrying him back toward the retreating command. Most of the time the Chinese stayed well back from the two Marines serving as rearguard but kept up a steady harassing fire throughout the morning.

In an hour the rescuers carried their burden a little more than one mile. Butler grew so accustomed to the snarl of bullets he hardly noticed them, but the pain in his arms and the dryness in his mouth and throat tortured him fiercely.

They covered 7 miles in 4 hours, and were about to give out when 25 Marines dropped back from the main command to keep the Boxers off their trail. Butler ordered them to prepare a stretcher from a poncho, which made the traveling easier. The rescuers carried the wounded man 12 miles that day, before catching up with the rest of the command at the bivouac site of the previous night. Here they camped again.

The four enlisted men who helped rescue Carter received Medals of Honor, but Marine officers were not eligible for the award until 1914. Butler and Lieutenant Harding were breveted for gallantry in action, later receiving the Brevet Medal. For officers, this ranked second only to the Medal of Honor they could not get. Had Butler been eligible for the top award then, his two later Medals of Honor would have given him three.

An additional 2,500 British, Russian and Italian troops reached the bivouac the next morning. The combined force of 3,000 again set out for Tientsin. Village by village, the force moved slowly, choked and blinded by a dust storm. Boxers contested them every mile and at every village. The dust chewed the skin off Butler's face, and his boots rubbed the skin off his heels. He never felt so miserable, nor so glad when the day ended with the Marines taking refuge in some filthy mud huts near the railroad. He settled his men, then collapsed in one of the miserable huts.

About noon the next day the allied force crossed a log jam in the river and fought its way into Tientsin. As the Peking legation had greeted the first foreign troops to arrive there, the Tientsin foreigners — 1,700 soldiers and a few hundred civilians — also cheered this force as saviors. But even with the new force, there was a total of only 4,700 fighting men against 500,000 fanatics fighting for their own ground and city.

Still, the 3,000 new arrivals rested only one day and marched out toward Peking, hunting the now missing relief force of Admiral Seymour. At noon the next day, they found the force only six miles away in the Shiku Arsenal. It doesn't appear that Butler and McCloy met here, or at Vera Cruz 14 years later.

The next morning both relief forces pulled out for Tientsin, setting fire to the arsenal as they left. A chain of explosions sounded behind the force all the way back. Neither Boxer nor Imperial soldier would be able to use those weapons to kill Americans.

The next task facing the forces in Tientsin was to lift the siege of the foreign compound located outside the old walled city of one million Chinese. Additional foreign troops dribbled in from the coast, but the combined forces could do nothing more than hold their position until 12 July when they numbered 7,000. That night the allies bombarded the city, then attacked it the next morning at various points.

Butler led his company to the outer mud wall, about 20 feet high with sloping sides, at 3 a.m. They climbed to the crest and halted there. Between this wall and the inner high stone wall lay 1,500 yards of open area. The Chinese had used the water from a network of canals to flood the space between the walls.

The Marines waited here until first light, while artillery hammered at the stone wall. Some of Butler's men cheered each time a shell ripped into the stone wall or landed beyond it in the city proper.

About seven in the morning, the Marines scrambled over the crest of the mud wall and charged across the water covered area, more concerned with the slowness of their progress than with the rifle balls whistling around them. The only protection was afforded by the slight banks of the rice paddies. Butler struggled from one bank to another, keeping his men firing and moving forward. The closer they got to the stone wall, the heavier the firing from the defenders grew.

As the Marines drew within easy firing range, more than a thousand Boxers and soldiers charged out of a gate to the left in an attempt to flank the attackers. Butler took 35 Marines and drove the enemy back, then rejoined the main force. He stopped long enough to pick up one of the wounded men and felt a bullet burn its way through his right thigh — the first of many wounds he would suffer in various battles. He missed the end of the two-day fight for Tientsin, a fight which saw the international force rout the Chinese and lift the siege.

While recovering from his wound, Butler celebrated his nineteenth birthday and his promotion to captain the same day. The promotion resulted from his brevet earned by rescuing Private Carter. Though still limping 3 weeks later — 4 August — he insisted on going with the 18,000 troops of 8 nations to relieve Peking. Six hundred American Marines joined the march. For Butler, the lust for battle was growing.

Junks carried the reserve ammunition and supplies, and pack mules the immediate needs, since the railroad was beyond quick repair and the line of march ran along the Pei-Ho River. The 6-mile-long force and its 6 miles of boats covered only 8 of the 80 miles the first day, suffering greatly from 140 degrees of heat and blinding dust churned up by the troops, cavalry horses and pack animals. Butler couldn't see beyond the Marines immediately ahead of him, nor did he really care to do so in that heat.

First combat broke out the next morning. Several thousand Boxers attacked the column, and quickly reeled back from more concentrated fire than they had ever encountered. Another massive attack came in the evening of 6 August, failing also before highly trained professional troops.

The torrid days stretched on, with progress slow. The

unhealed wound in his leg tortured Butler, but did not stop him from marching. Half the Marines dropped from the heat during the day, but revived enough in the cool evening to continue the next day. Before reaching Peking, 200 dropped out permanently. One died. Butler collapsed one afternoon from the heat, but in a few minutes resumed the march. Fortunately, attacks from the Boxers and Imperial soldiers dwindled down to harassing raids brushed aside by the relief force. Still, it took 10 days to march 80 miles.

The four columns of the command halted three miles from Peking 13 August, in a rainstorm that dropped temperatures to a merciful level. The great battlemented wall around the city stretched for miles north and south. Inside waited 50,000 fanatics.

The attack on the city started about 3 a.m., 13 August and soon carried the forces into the Chinese City, south of the Tartar City. As Butler led his company through a gate, a bullet struck a button on his blouse, driving the ring of the button into his chest. The bullet glanced off, but the force spun Butler around and knocked him flat. His head struck something, knocking him out for several minutes. For the rest of the day he was too weak to take part in the fighting.

The relief force drove the last of the fanatics from the city by noon the next day, 15 August, ending the siege and the Boxer Rebellion. Twenty-six of Butler's company were killed or wounded, and others incapacitated by heat. And though Butler didn't get the medal he should have earned because of the campaign, there would be other wars.

Butler came home from Peking to recover from his wounds, serving two years at the Philadelphia Navy Yard. Then he took a battalion of Marines to Panama when another revolt flared up briefly. This was the beginning of a long feud with the Navy brass. Butler believed admirals bore grudges against non-academy officers and all Marines. Every time he thought his men were mistreated in some way, he howled loud enough to be heard in Washington.

In Panama, Butler's battalion was ordered to install coastal guns in their "spare time." Butler claimed the admiral in command accused the Marines of laziness when malaria felled so many they didn't complete the project quickly enough to suit him. Then the admiral sent twice as many sailors ashore and the Marines outworked them, according to Butler. The admiral still ordered the Marines to work harder. Furious, Butler complained to his congressman father, then chairman of the House Naval Affairs Committee. Papa's intervention caused the admiral to ease up, but it also made Butler a marked man in some quarters. The more he yelled, the more trouble he reaped. The military has never taken kindly to political intervention in purely military affairs.

Butler earned another kind of reputation during those years. His flair for showmanship and his raw courage made him a natural for taking on two-bit Latin generals in the "banana wars." The press found him good copy as they took note of his escapades.

Returning to Philadelphia for another tour of duty, Butler married Ethel Peters in June 1905, a marriage he never regretted. They left immediately for the Philippines for two years duty and honeymooning.

The organized portion of the Philippine Insurrection was over by then, so the duty was not rigorous. Butler commanded a company at Olongapo Navy Yard 60 miles north of Manila. His daughter, Ethel, was born there 2 November 1906. Recurring malaria forced Butler to take 9 months sick leave in 1908. But idleness was not for him. He took over management of a near-bankrupt coal mine in West Virginia and turned it into a profitable business. But a couple of mine accidents left him so battered that Mrs. Butler agreed he should go back to war. It wasn't so bloody there, she said.

Back on duty in Philadelphia, Butler was promoted to major in 1909. His son, Smedley, was born there 12 July 1909. Then he took command of a battalion of Marines operating out of Panama from 1909 to 1914, a mobile spearhead of forces that put down revolts in the Caribbean.

The first of three expeditions to Nicaragua came in the spring of 1910, but didn't amount to much for the Marines so they returned to Panama. But a week after his family joined him there, Butler left with his battalion again for Nicaragua, this time for four months. He found the rebel force of 350 men, supported by the United States, surrounded by 1,500 government troops in the city of Bluefield. The rebels were about finished, until Butler pulled one of the stunts for which he was becoming famous. He sent word to the government generals that the Marines were there only to protect American lives. To do this, he must insist that their troops leave their guns outside the town when they attacked the rebels. He would station Marines at the edge of town to make sure the troops didn't bring in weapons.

The generals protested they couldn't take the town without guns. Disarm the rebels also, they urged. No, Butler said, the rebels would be firing outward, so they wouldn't endanger American lives. Only those firing inward constituted a threat.

The generals exploded at the impossible terms Butler handed them, but they didn't feel up to taking on the Marines. They gave up the siege and left, and their army soon fell apart, forcing their government to do the same.

The third expedition to Nicaragua started in August

1912, when the entire country was in a civil war. Butler's battalion, 11 officers and 350 Marines, supported the government this time, ending the revolt in 3 months by winning a couple of tough battles.

War with Mexico loomed in 1914, over a border dispute. In addition, the new Mexican president, General Huerta, had a strong hatred of Yankees. When shooting appeared imminent, Butler was sent to Mexico City as a spy, nearly losing his life.

Butler took his battalion to Mexico in January 1914, aboard the battleship **Minnesota**. Half a dozen American warships were anchored in the bay at Vera Cruz when they arrived. Butler joined the staff of Admiral Frank Fletcher during this period of "watchful waiting" for the war.

Butler didn't do much waiting, though. The Admiral needed him for a secret mission to Mexico City, and the flamboyant major quickly agreed. Wearing civilian clothes, he boarded the Admiral's barge on Sunday night and went into Vera Cruz. Here he crept aboard the private railroad car of the superintendent of the line, a co-conspirator in the spy plot.

The next day the train bumped along the tracks toward Mexico City. The American legation head introduced him as a secret service man in Mexico seeking an escaped American criminal believed to be serving in the Mexican Army. This story got him the cooperation of the Mexican secret servicemen who escorted him to various army posts in the capital area. While supposedly looking at men, he observed carefully the posts and fortifications and drew up maps each night in the home of the railroad superintendent.

True to the Butler sense of humor, the picture of the "American criminal" he supposedly was seeking was in reality a picture of a fellow Marine officer, one he claimed looked like a desperado.

Butler's greatest achievement during the ten days was a tour of the royal palace built over an old fort. The American Charge d'Affaires, Nelson O'Shaughnessy, was friendly with President Huerta, despite the strained relations between the two countries. O'Shaughnessy arranged for the secret service help for Butler to look over the palace. Butler didn't get to see the old fort underneath, but he saw that the palace itself couldn't withstand much artillery pounding.

At the end of the ten days, the Mexican secret servicemen became suspicious of Butler's prolonged search and his interest in purely military installations. Butler immediately took the train for Vera Cruz, tailed by two of the agents. Just before reaching the coast, he went to the washroom and jumped out of the window.

In the darkness Butler hurried to the American consulate where he signaled the flagship in the harbor to send a boat for him. Then he went to the docks to wait for the boat. There a group of Mexicans jumped him. Likely they only wanted his money, clothes and suitcase, but the maps inside the bag were enough to get him shot. The wiry Butler slugged, kicked and cussed while the mob ripped and pounded at him, smashing his face and body. He was just about finished when the American boat landed, and a boatswain's bull voice called out to him. The Mexicans moved back a short distance and Butler ran to the boat. The sailors wanted to take on the gang, but for once Butler had had his fill of fighting. He wanted only to get his maps to the Admiral.

A full war with Mexico never did develop, so Butler's mission was wasted. He was aboard the cruiser **USS Chester** at Tampico when word arrived of the Vera Cruz landing. The skipper of the old ship ran her at top speed — 21 knots. Like Butler, he was afraid the fighting would end before they could get there.

The **Chester** squeezed through the narrow breakwater into Vera Cruz harbor about 11 p.m., 21 April, missing the first day of battle. But sporadic rifle fire still sounded at various points in the city.

Before midnight, Butler was ordered to land with his one company of Marines and one of sailors, using the whaleboats towed by Chief Boatswain McCoy's motor launches. He reported in to Colonel Buck Neville in the railroad terminal. The Colonel ordered him to place his men on the line near the roundhouse.

With first light the landing force began its sweep to take over the entire city. Snipers and machine guns opposed them from rooftops and inside houses. A company of seamen coming down the middle of a street were cut down by rooftop machine guns. So, the Marines used a different system. They smashed their way into the first house of a block, chopped a hole in the common wall with the next house and killed its occupants. Then they chopped a hole into the common wall with the next adjoining house. When all houses of the block were cleared, they climbed up on the flat roofs and shot the snipers up there.

Once, two of Butler's men charged into a deserted house and were shot down from below. He ordered several others to fire their weapons into the floor, then they pulled up the planking. Two dead Mexicans were found under the floor.

House to house, the Marines fought through the day. Near the outskirts of the city, a larger group of well-hidden snipers kept some of Butler's men pinned down behind scant cover in the middle of a street. They couldn't even tell where the firing was coming from and none of the Marines seemed willing to try and find out. This wasn't the Marine way of doing battle, so Butler armed himself with only a swagger stick and calmly walked along the road, pointing out sniper positions with the stick. How many rounds were fired at him from huts and ditches, overturned wagons and piles of rubble, will never be known. Nor can anyone say how the snipers missed him at that range.

Butler's calm stroll with only a swagger stick, and with disregard to heavy enemy fire, soon brought the Marines charging the positions, a sight that doesn't help the aim of even seasoned regular troops. In this case, the Marines cleaned out the green irregulars without losing a man.

Vera Cruz was the first combat in which Marine *officers* were eligible for the Medal of Honor. Accordingly, Butler received his first medal there. He "was eminent and conspicuous in command of his battalion. He exhibited courage and skill in leading his men throughout the action."

Butler refused to accept the medal on the grounds that he didn't deserve it. The Navy Department not only gave it to him, but ordered him to accept and wear it. That ended the matter.

The Haiti campaign in 1915, came next for the flamboyant Butler. He led the 26-man patrol that located and captured two of the three strongholds of the Cacos there (Author's note: for details, see Chapter Eleven), Fort Capois and Fort Dipitie. That left only one stronghold, Fort Riviere, headquarters of the top leaders of the bandits. Capturing it would end organized insurrection in the country.

Higher brass thought it would take at least 1,000 Marines to storm the old French fort. Butler volunteered to attack it with 100 men. The brass allowed it, and he hand-picked 3 companies of Marines — 25 men each — and a company of 25 bluejackets.

Butler sent two companies of Marines up the main trail toward the fort, the bluejackets along a second path, and led the other company of Marines up a third mountainous trail, which was barely a path. The detachments were supposed to arrive at 7 a.m., 17 November 1915. Each trail ended on a different side of the fort perched atop a mountain peak. Butler halted his company at the edge of some woods at the appointed hour, then studied the thick brick walls of the fort 100 feet above where he stood. About 200 yards of rocky, steep slope separated the woods and fort, without a bit of cover. The fort was about 200 feet square, with walls 15 to 30 feet high depending on the contour of the land.

Butler could detect no sign of life inside the fort, nor could he tell if the other companies had arrived. Assigning half his company for cover fire with machine guns, he blew his whistle for the attack at 7:30 a.m. Heads popped up along the wall, bringing the instant chatter of machine guns from Butler's base of fire. The heads vanished. Butler led the charge up the steep and rocky slope, and from the higher position could see the other companies. They couldn't charge their walls as planned because the other slopes were too steep. The French who built the fort had made the slopes that way for just that purpose.

Despite this, and despite growing fire from the walls, Butler staggered on toward the entrance in the south wall. Once he turned his ankle and fell, but bounded up again and lurched on over the uneven rocky surface.

The Cacos couldn't stop Butler, but the entrance in the wall did. It no longer existed. A brick wall stood where the gate should have been. Butler hesitated only a moment, then trotted along the wall, hunting another opening. The Cacos had to get in and out somewhere.

Machine gunners did their job so well hardly any shots splattered near Butler's men now. He found the entrance in some underbrush well down the wall: a drain about three feet wide and four feet high. He peeked inside and saw it ended about 15 feet inside the fort. But a brick wall nearly blocked the far end, and a single guard behind that wall snapped a quick shot at Butler. He jerked back, trying to figure a way to get through.

Sergeant Ross Iams of Gransville, Pennsylvania, waited a few seconds, then said, "Oh, hell, I'm going through." Then he started into the drain. Private Sam Gross (real last name Marguiles) of Philadelphia beat out Butler for second place, and the three of them crawled like someone was fanning their tails instead of waiting ahead. The guard fired into the drain, somehow missing all three Marines, though they nearly filled the space. Then Iams killed the guard.

The trio burst out inside the fort to find themselves facing about 60 half-naked, howling Cacos charging them, throwing spears and rocks, firing rifles and swinging machetes. The three Marines shot the frontrunners, then used rifle butts and bayonets. The rest of Butler's men came in through the drain to ease the pressure. A couple of minutes later, the other two detachments scaled the now undefended walls. Vicious in-fighting followed for the next 15 minutes, ending with 60 Cacos dead or prisoner and only a few minor wounds for the Marines.

Butler then used a ton of dynamite to blast down the walls of the fort. That ended organized resistance in Haiti for several years. Iams, Gross and Butler all received a Medal of Honor for their part in the assault, it being Butler's second award.

For two years Butler remained in Haiti, organizing and training a native constabulary to maintain law and order. Now a lieutenant colonel in the U.S. Marines, he also was commandant and major general of the Haitain Gendarmerie. The Marines under Butler also held double ranks. They made the Gendarmerie a first class military-police force of 2,500 men.

When World War I broke out, Butler flooded Washington with requests for duty in France. But he had too many enemies in high places. Now a colonel, he was assigned to Quantico, Virginia, in charge of training other Marines for combat. The war was nearly over before he finally managed to get transferred to France. Promoted to brigadier general at the age of 38 in 1918 — the youngest Marine ever to hold the rank — he was placed in command of a pest hole known as Camp Pontanezen, in Brest, France. The camp was one big filthy mud hole without sanitation or housing except the tents the occupants brought with them. Hundreds died daily of the flu.

Butler fumed at the lack of a combat command, but he converted the camp into the finest in France, saving thousands of lives. For this he received Distinguished Service Medals from both the Army and Navy, and the Legion of Honor from France. He would have traded all three for a week on the front lines.

Butler became a major general, but he continued his feuding with military and civilian brass in Washington. He was arrested once for uncomplimentary remarks made about Mussolini, the first general to have such a thing happen since the Civil War. The charges were later dropped.

In 1931, Butler was the senior marine general, in line for the post of commandant of the corps, but his many years of outspoken conduct cost him the appointment. President Hoover promoted another officer over him. Butler then retired at the age of 50, with 33 years service, 14 battles and 17 medals to his credit. In 1942, a destroyer was given his name. He died in 1940, when 58 years old, in the Philadelphia Naval Hospital.

THIRTEENTH DOUBLE WINNER Smedley Butler.

CHAPTER FOURTEEN

John King
(1865-1938)

The Navy's only double winner of the Medal of Honor from "below decks" was a career sailor with 7 consecutive enlistments, totaling more than 23 years of unbroken service aboard 15 battleships and cruisers. John King, born 7 February 1865, in Ireland, emigrated to New York before enlisting for the first time 20 July 1893, as a coal passer. This was the dirtiest and meanest job on a ship in that era, shoveling coal into the furnaces that heated the boilers which powered the engines of the ships.

For the most part, King was somewhat typical of the bluejackets of his day. But 4 consecutive good conduct awards covering 20 years made him somewhat unique, an Irishman and a sailor who stayed out of trouble.

During most of his first enlistment, King served aboard the battleship **New York**, shoveling coal. She patrolled the South Atlantic and West Indies waters. King worked up to fireman second class, fireman first class and oiler.

King's second enlistment proved more exciting. He was an oiler in the engine rooms of the battleship **Massachusetts** when the Spanish-American War started. She was one of four new battleships — the Navy's first "first class" dreadnoughts — around which the American fleet was built. More than 10,000 tons each, monsters for that era, they could steam at nearly 17 knots. Each carried four 13-inch, eight 8-inch and four 6-inch guns.

The **Massachusetts** left Norfolk, Virginia, 13 May 1898, with the "Flying Squadron" of Commodore Schley, for the blockade of Cuba. The squadron — three battleships and a cruiser at first — blockaded Ceinfuegos, Cuba, from 22 to 28 May, then moved on to Santiago harbor. Here four battleships formed an outer ring four miles from the entrance to the harbor, to prevent the Spanish fleet from escaping. Three picket launches formed an inner line halfway to the harbor, about two miles out. The ring of ships pulled in a little closer at night, and one of the battleships kept its searchlights trained on the harbor mouth.

King got his first taste of combat 31 May 1898. The **Massachusetts**, battleship **Iowa** and cruiser **New Orleans** steamed in to within 7,000 yards of the harbor entrance, crossing it at about ten knots. The main batteries opened fire on the forts guarding the harbor and on the Spanish ship **Cristobal Colon** anchored near the entrance.

Naval combat holds a special kind of terror for those below decks. Each time a 13-inch gun fired, 520 pounds of powder exploded. Hearing this without seeing what was happening caused the senses to imagine all kinds of horrors, greater than actually could be seen above decks. King coped with this fear by concentrating on the operation of the huge engines. He also found some comfort in the fact that steel gratings were laid across the hatches to prevent shells from plunging below decks through the openings. Also, the ship carried 18-inch armor plating on her sides. Fortunately, the gun and deck crews kept up a rapid commentary of what they saw, in great detail. King could follow the course of battle by listening to them.

Shell fire from the **Massachusetts** soon drove the **Cristobal Colon** into the inner harbor to avoid destruction. Then all batteries concentrated on the forts, which returned the fire triple-fold. That was the purpose of the bombardment, to determine the big-gun strength of the Spanish.

Shells splashed all round the **Massachusetts** without a single hit. After ten minutes of continuous volleys, she ceased firing and steamed seaward. The Spanish kept up their bombardment until she was well out of range.

For the next 33 days, the squadron continued its blockade outside the harbor, occasionally going in closer to bombard the coastal defenses then steaming out again. For King the main problem during this time was the heat in the engine room. The Spanish Fleet could attempt to flee at any moment, so the blockaders had to be prepared for battle constantly. This meant each ship was kept coaled to capacity, its furnaces hot, with half the ships moving east across the harbor entrance and half moving west so that no matter what direction the enemy might attempt to flee half the ships would be ready to follow.

All this meant the heat in the engine room was up to 130 degrees at night and up to 150 degrees in the middle of the day. Often those nearest the furnaces and boilers passed out from the heat and had to be carried topside to revive.

The next big change in strategy came 3 July. The **Massachusetts** pulled out of formation about 4 a.m. and steamed to Guantanamo Bay 37 miles eastward, to load up with coal. When she returned the next day, the crew learned the Spanish Fleet had attempted to flee Santiago the morning of 3 July and was sunk by the squadron.

King complained as loudly as the rest of the crew over missing the biggest battle they would ever get a chance to fight. But that night they received a minor consolation prize. A Spanish cruiser came steaming out of the inner harbor to the entrance, where her crew tried to sink her to block the narrow channel. The **Massachusetts** steamed in at full speed, main batteries blasting. The first round pierced all the way through the cruiser. Accuracy of the fire, as well as from two other ships now steaming in, frightened the Spanish crew into abandoning ship before sinking her. She ran aground at one side, failing to block the channel.

Three weeks later the **Massachusetts** steamed through the minefields of Guanica Harbor, Puerto Rico, for the landing and occupation of the island after mild opposition from shore batteries. Then she sailed home to New York 20 August 1898. King received a Sampson Medal and Spanish Campaign Medal for the Cuba and Puerto Rico operations.

Four ships and three years later found King a watertender aboard the cruiser **Vicksburg**, fighting the Philippine Insurrection. This part of his career would have passed unnoticed except for a chance occurence.

Insurgent Filipinos, who had fought the Spanish for years, turned on the United States after she acquired the Philippines from Spain in 1898. Most of the native citizens had no intention of trading Spanish colonial rule for Yankee rule. Under their leader, General Aguinaldo, the rebels fought on for more than two additional years.

For King, this meant long hours of duty in the boiler and engine rooms keeping the **Vicksburg** patroling the coastal waters and occasionally offering fire support to ground troops ashore.

In March 1901, the unusual delegation of an American general, four American officers and close to a hundred native Filipinos boarded the **Vicksburg** in Manila amid great secrecy. Once they were aboard, none of the crew was allowed to leave the ship. It wasn't until the ship cleared the bay and started north up the coast of Luzon that King learned the natives were Macabee scouts, natives of the Macabee province of Luzon who once served as the civil guard under the Spanish. Now, dressed as guerrillas, they were helping the Americans. Their mission remained secret, however.

On the night of 14 March, the **Vicksburg** steamed in close to the shore of an isolated part of Luzon. The special force went ashore in small craft and the **Vicksburg** headed back toward Manila. None of the crew knew what was planned ashore.

Eleven days later, the **Vicksburg** returned to the same spot in time to pick up the special force. When they boarded the **Vicksburg**, they brought a prisoner.

And what a prisoner!

King then learned the Macabee scouts had gone ashore, posing as guerrillas bringing in five American prisoners. They marched into the stronghold of General Aguinaldo, captured and brought him back. It was hard to believe the prisoner was the great Aguinaldo. The small, impassive youth seemed hardly old enough to be out of school, had he ever gone to one. And he certainly showed none of the toughness that had held the insurrection together for so long. His capture cut the heart out of organized resistance in the Philippines, though sporadic fighting continued for several years.

The **Vicksburg** steamed back to Manila at flank speed, putting the old boilers under severe strain. Once there, the special force and its prisoner went ashore. The **Vicksburg** returned to patrol duty, but not for long. The long months of constant steaming and frequent high speed runs had kept the boilers and engines strained beyond their limit. The final high speed run down the coast had worried King every knot of the way. Now, a valve ruptured, causing immediate danger of a boiler exploding and destroying the ship.

King ordered the compartment cleared while he stayed

behind to make emergency repairs. Steam soon filled the viciously hot room, raising temperatures to an unbearable level. But King stayed there anyway, knowing that if he failed he would lose his ship and many of her crew.

At times King had to close his eyes against the stinging steam and work by feel. Barely able to breathe, he stayed with his task until the repairs were made and the danger eased.

For this act, King received his first Medal of Honor and a Philippine Campaign medal.

King continued service in the Asiatic Squadron on several ships, until returning to New York in 1903. Nine years on various ships in the Atlantic followed. He was aboard the **USS Salem** 13 September 1909, when another accident in the boiler room demanded an instance of maximum sacrifice from King.

With steam rapidly filling the room, King ordered all others to go topside. The crewmen were quite happy to let him have the place to himself. Steam spewed out of the damaged boiler itself, the worst kind of repair to attempt.

But skills acquired during 16 years below decks gave King confidence. He first hauled the hot coals from the furnace heating the boiler to an explosive level. This kept the pressure from building higher, but did not lessen it immediately. Then, groping his way through the steam, he went to work on the boiler. Even with eyes squinted open whenever he could stand it, he had trouble seeing what he was doing. But he made the repair and the crisis passed.

For this last effort, King received his second Medal of Honor. Seventeen days later he was promoted to chief watertender.

King was on the battleship **Florida** when she went to Vera Cruz in 1914, for the watchful waiting, then the landing and occupation of the city. Now nearly 50 years old, he figured this to be his last campaign.

The old chief was transferred to the Fleet Naval Reserve and released from active duty 26 December 1916. During World War I, he was recalled for another 28 months at the New York receiving station where he trained new sailors. He retired again 3 November 1923, and died 20 May 1938.

Naval History Photograph

FOURTEENTH DOUBLE WINNER John King.

San Francisco Maritime Museum

FOURTEENTH DOUBLE WINNER John King served aboard this ship, the USS VICKSBURG, when he earned his first Medal of Honor in 1901.

U. S. Naval Historical Center Photograph

A SECOND VIEW of the USS VICKSBURG.

FOURTEENTH DOUBLE WINNER John King earned his second medal below decks of this ship, the USS SALEM.

CHAPTER FIFTEEN

Ernest A. Janson
(1878-1930)

The last five double winners of the Medal of Honor, all enlisted Marines, earned their decorations knocking out German machine guns in World War I. They also were unique in that each received a Medal of Honor from the Navy and one from the Army for *a single act of valor each*. Why these five, and only these five, should be decorated twice with the highest award, for only one heroic deed each, is something of a mystery.

An additional mystery hangs over the first of the quintet, Ernest August Janson, because he served his country under the alias of Charles F. Hoffman. Explanations of this offered by various writers appear to be rather poor guesswork.

Born 17 August 1878, in New York, Janson began ten years army service in 1900. For seven years he served aboard various ships and shore stations, landing in France in June 1917. A half-pint gunnery sergeant like Dan Daly, he was just as quiet and just as tough. But Daly looked like a bulldog ready to do battle while Janson's thin face seemed mild, even a bit sad. Still, he couldn't have been a professional soldier for 18 years, nor been a Marine gunnery sergeant, without having iron will when it was needed.

A prelude to the battle for Belleau Wood came early the morning of 6 June 1918, two miles west of the forest. Two companies of the Fifth Marines formed 4 ranks about 800 yards long at 3:45 a.m. Janson made each of his men check his Springfield rifle, then watched quietly for 15 minutes while artillery pounded their objective, a low hill listed on the chart as Hill 142. Scrawny pines dotted the hill about a thousand yards to the northeast. In between the hill and Janson, a wheat field sloped up gently. Red poppies here and there stood out sharply against the green wheat. Janson couldn't see the German machine gun nests hidden in the tree clumps and small ravines.

At first light, the signal came to move out. Janson waved his men forward and scrambled over the top with them. They moved only 50 yards before German guns shattered the silence, driving them to the ground, hugging dirt. Janson didn't stay down long, though. Hiding in the wheat field was no place for a Marine. The fire came from a clump of trees up ahead. When the captain shouted for them to charge, Janson snapped the order to his men and off they went. Marines died in the rush, but the survivors overran the German position.

Janson led his men through the trees to the open wheat field on the far side. Fire from a second wooded area brought the Marines charging again, with the same result. Then Hill 142 loomed just ahead, with machine guns chattering down at the Marines. Half the remaining Marines fell rushing the hill. The others took the position in minutes and drove on beyond. Then they returned to the northern slope and dug in.

A full battalion of German infantry counter-attacked before the trenches were ready, but the sharp-shooting Marines drove them back. Then German artillery pounded the slope while infantry tried three more times to retake the position. Janson kept his Springfield hot, pausing only long enough to make certain his men maintained a steady fire.

In a short lull that followed the fourth attack, Janson moved his men to a better position and put them to work digging in. Then he spotted a dozen Germans crawling through the brush nearby, dragging five machine guns with them. Those guns could wipe out what remained of the two companies.

Janson shouted a warning, grabbed his rifle and charged. He didn't even try shooting the Germans. Like many others in World War I, he seemed to regard his Springfield — first and foremost — as something to hold his bayonet. Holding the weapon in front of him at the ready, he speared the nearest German through the chest. Pulling his bayonet free, he lunged at a second man, killing him also. Then a bullet hit Janson in the chest, spinning him around. He stayed on his feet and charged the other ten Germans. The diminutive size of Janson couldn't have scared the Germans, but when they saw that cold steel coming at them they fled, leaving all five machine guns behind. The Marines retained possession of Hill 142.

Though severely wounded and out of the war, Janson survived to receive Medals of Honor from both the Army and Navy, plus the French Medaille Militaire and Montenegan Silver Medal, the Portuguese Crus de Guerra, and Italian Crose di Guerre.

For several months Janson lay in the U.S. Naval Hospital in New York. When recovered, he spent seven years there as a recruiter for the Marine Corps. Retiring as a sergeant major in September 1926, he lived in Long Island until his death 14 May 1930. He was buried in Brooklyn.

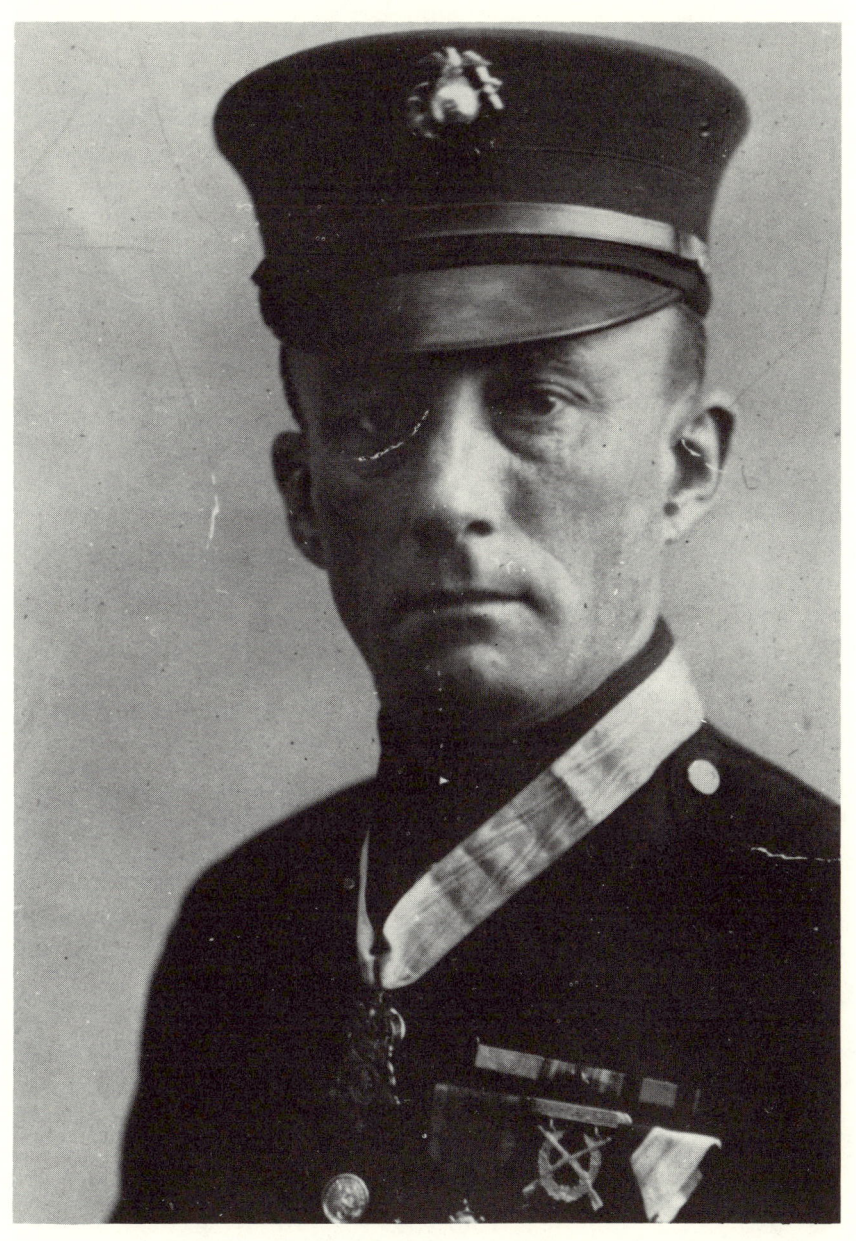

Official U. S. Marine Corps Photo

FIFTEENTH DOUBLE WINNER *Ernest A. Janson.*

CHAPTER SIXTEEN

Matej Kocak
(1882-1918)

His comrades at arms claimed Matej Kocak loved fighting above all else — not so much the danger as the competition, man against man in mortal combat proving who was best. If so, he enjoyed his life's work and was in sympathetic company, as a U.S. Marine.

Born 31 December 1882, in Egbell, Hungary (sometimes Austria), Kocak emigrated to New York in 1906, when he was 24 years old. Stories about the leathernecks in Cuba, China and the Philippines lured him into the Marine Corps in 1907. He never left it, nor ever wanted to. He learned to speak English but never lost his heavy Germanic accent — but an accent was not uncommon in the Marine Corps of his day. Most of his service was on foreign soil anyway.

Kocak learned his "trade" in the various skirmishes of the Marines in the ten years preceeding World War I. His finest effort came in the Dominican Republic in 1916.

Anarchy caused by frequent insurrection reined in the Dominican Republic from 1899 to 1916. When the current president was forced from office by another revolt in May 1916, the U.S. sent in seamen and Marines to snuff out the rebellion and occupy the country. This was the only way to prevent European debtor countries from intervening in the Western Hemisphere in violation of the Monroe Doctrine.

The Marines chased the rebels across the country, defeating them in battle each time they stopped along the route. Kocak proved to be the most aggressive of the Marines. The sudden chatter of rifle fire would send others seeking cover, but Kocak would charge the nearest enemy position, killing or driving out the rebels he found there. For his courage he received his corporal's stripes, a rank he claimed was equal to an Army or Navy lieutenant.

Kocak went to France in 1918, with the 66th Rifle Company, Fifth Marines. In June, the regiment fought its way into Marine Corps legend in the battle for Belleau Wood. Kocak earned his sergeant's stripes there.

After the battle, the regiment rested a few days in a small village, amidst rumors the men might get leave in Paris. But the high command had different plans for them.

The final German offensive of the war — 28 May to 4 June — had driven three big bulges in the western front, at Amiens, Saint Mihiel, and Chateau-Thierry. The tip of the latter was pinched off at Belleau Wood by the Marines. In mid-July they were called on to help cut off the entire salient.

To achieve tactical surprise, 70,000 French and American troops were not moved to the front until just before the counter-offensive. For that reason, also, the Marines didn't even know where they were going when they marched out of their rest camp 16 July 1918. But they soon knew they were not going to Paris. The sound of the big guns grew louder pretty quickly.

Odd looking French trucks, with tiny wheels and no springs, carried the Marines over what passed for roads, through the night of 16-17 July. They quit the trucks the next morning, and, without sleep, marched past midafternoon. Resting a couple of hours, they moved on at dark.

About 10 p.m. a thunderstorm broke, soaking them and turning the road into a quagmire. Fully rested soldiers would have found it tough going. Men who had gone without sleep for two days and nights should have given up. The Marines grumbled, but kept going. The line of march took them into a forest hiding a massive army.

Kocak saw more tanks, artillery, mules and men than ever before. He still didn't know where they were going; but the brass could worry about that. He just hoped the Krauts didn't catch them with artillery or gas while they were in the forest.

Early in the morning, word came down the column that they would be late reaching the line in time for the attack. The Marines, after an incredible two and a half days of forced travel without sleep, started double-timing when they heard the opening barrage ahead. They were in the Retz Forest near Villers-Cotterets south of Soissons.

The final half-mile to the jump-off line took the Fifth Marines up a steep hill. The Sixth Marines dropped back with the reserves, cursing their luck. The 35-year-old Kocak forced himself to keep up with the younger leathernecks despite his weary legs.

From the top of the last hill, Kocak could see the line ahead, but the barrage had stopped and the attack started without the Fifth in place. Kocak unleashed the Marine yell and others joined him; it didn't take them long to catch up. German machine guns chattered in the distance almost immediately, but the outposts were only lightly manned. Tactical surprise had been achieved.

Swiftly Kocak led his squad across a waist-high wheat field. He saw Cukela off to his left just as machine guns opened up from a small farm house ahead and a ravine to the left. Cukela sent his men to both sides of the ravine to silence the gun there, while Kocak led a charge on the farm house. A corporal shouldered through a side door and disappeared inside. The bark of his Springfield, followed by silence, ended the threat from that point.

The first encounter set the pattern for the day. Across fields and around ravines, through villages and farm buildings the Marines battled. Each time they encountered a machine gun nest, the men meeting it head on dropped to the ground and behind whatever cover they could find. Those on each side flanked the position and knocked it out with grenades, rifle fire or bayonets. Usually they encountered a second machine gun providing cover fire for the first.

Finally, the inevitable happened. One machine gun nest about two hundred yards ahead thinned the ranks of the Marines. Kocak couldn't even see the gun in the rough ground, scrub trees and heavy underbrush, and there didn't seem to be any way to flank it. The entire battalion had to find cover while the officers tried to figure a way to knock out the gun. Kocak gave no thought to grand strategy. From his position a little to the right of the gun, he crawled forward toward the general area from which the rapid fire spewed.

Kocak still couldn't see the gun, but its chatter led him ever closer. He hugged the ground, knowing he was dead if the Germans spotted him. When he figured he was slightly behind the position, but not far enough for the second gun to spot him, he jumped up and charged the sound.

Three Germans manning the gun didn't see Kocak until he was almost ready to lunge. When they did spot him, they darted away from the position so fast Kocak didn't get to kill any of them. But they left their machine gun behind.

Kocak signaled the battalion to come on, just as he heard the back-up machine gun cut loose at him. He dropped to the ground and crawled out of there like a blue racer snake. Man, could he crawl, his friends joshed him.

In the protection of the woods, Kocak encountered about 25 French colonial troops, tough little Moroccans who loved to get in close enough to Germans to use their long knives. They could dissect a German in 30 seconds, stringing his guts over a tree limb.

Since his accent sounded very much like that of a German, Kocak communicated with sign language. He motioned for about half the Moroccans to flank him from the left and he led the others to the right. About 20 feet from the gun, he halted a moment, thinking about the Moroccans and their knives. Then he removed his bayonet and laid his rifle aside. With a signal to the others, he jumped up and charged. Seven startled Germans saw the wild Marine and dusky-skinned Moroccans coming, and swung their machine gun around as they fired. Several Moroccans dropped, but all the Germans died from a slash or thrust of a knife or bayonet.

For this action, Kocak received a Medal of Honor from both the Army and Navy. Three months later he was killed in action at Blanc Mont Ridge.

SIXTEENTH DOUBLE WINNER Matej Kocak.

SIXTEENTH DOUBLE WINNER Matej Kocak (far right) is shown with three unknown Marines.

CHAPTER SEVENTEEN

Louis Cukela
(1888-1956)

Although he butchered the King's English, Louis Cukela had little trouble communicating with the Marines who served under him during his 30 years in the Corps. His colorful expressions became legend.

Born 1 May 1888, in Spalato, Serbia (sometimes Austria), Cukela was educated there. He and a brother emigrated to Minneapolis in 1913. A year later he joined the U.S. Army, but after two years he purchased his discharge. He then enlisted in the Marines 31 January 1917.

With his educational background, previous Army service, and a war soon in progress, Cukela's rank jumped to gunnery sergeant by the summer of 1918. He went to France with the same outfit as Kocak, the 66th Rifle Company, Fifth Marines. A strict disciplinarian, he made his platoon the one Marine officers held up as the example for all others, a platoon of machine-like perfection and bull whip toughness. It matched his personality, even his appearance. He looked like a Prussian officer, with piercing eyes and stern square features made harsher by a heavy, neatly trimmed mustache.

Cukela's first big fight came at Belleau Wood, where he proved the wisdom of superior officers who had promoted him over those with longer service. His platoon was the crack outfit of the regiment.

But the really big moment of Cukela's life came 18 July 1918, only an hour or so after Kocak's similar performance, during the Soissons battle near the Forest de Retz, Villers-Cotterets. A German position well hidden in the wooded area held two machine guns which could swing around to cover any attempt to flank the position. The crusty sergeant studied the nest a few moments and made his decision. He was famous in the Marine Corps for his method of chewing out subordinates who failed to carry out their assignments.

"Next time I send a goddam fool, I go myself," Cukela would always say. Apparently he thought this was the time to send such a fool, because he began crawling forward, trying to keep a tree between himself and the snarling machine guns.

Some of his men shouted at Cukela, urging him to come back, but he concentrated his attention on the guns searching for him. Eventually the Germans lost sight of him in the trees, and he crawled around behind them. About 30 feet away, he saw the guns were in separate pits, with the crewmen glancing nervously in all directions. They knew he was close.

Like Janson, Kocak and others, Cukela preferred sticking 'em to shooting 'em, when the situation permitted. Instead of shooting now, he jumped up and charged with his gleaming steel ready at the end of his Springfield.

The Germans spotted him and cried out, but he was on them too quickly. He lunged forward and plunged his bayonet into the chest of one man, then pulled the steel free and slashed upward, gutting another while the third fled to the second gun pit.

Some grenades lay on the ground in a pool of blood spurting from the deboweled German. Cukela scooped up three of the slippery grenades and threw them at the other pit. While smoke boiled up from the bombed out position, he charged it. The four surviving Germans held up their arms in surrender. One of them shook his head and muttered, "Teufelhund" — "Devil Dog" — the German name for the American Marines who "killed everything that moved."

For this act, Cukela received his Medals of Honor, one each from the Army and the Navy.

The Sixth Marine Regiment, with the final two double winners of the medal, temporarily relieved the Fifth the next day. By early August, the Chateau-Thierry salient was removed. Both the Fifth and Sixth Marine Regiments went on to the battles of Saint Mihiel, Meuse Argonne and Blanc Mont Ridge.

Cukela suffered his first wound at Saint Mihiel, and his second in the Champagne sector, neither serious. Receiving a battlefield commission as second lieutenant 26 September 1918, he rose to first lieutenant in 1919, and captain in 1921.

In the post-World War I era, Cukela served at various Marine posts and zones in Haiti, Santo Domingo, the Philippines, China, and at stateside bases. Retiring with the rank of major in 1940, he was recalled the next month as World War II loomed, serving until 1946. He died 19 March 1956, in the U.S. Naval Hospital in Bethesda, Maryland.

SEVENTEENTH DOUBLE WINNER Louis Cukela.

CHAPTER EIGHTEEN

John Henry Pruitt (1896-1918)

By "old breed" Marine standards, John Henry Pruitt was just a green kid of 20 years when he joined the Corps. But in his brief period of service, he earned the admiration and respect of even the gruffest old leathernecks.

Born 4 October 1896, in Fayetteville, Arkansas, Pruitt enlisted 25 April 1917, in Arizona. Tall and blonde-haired, he had a deceptively mild appearance.

Pruitt left for France 19 January 1918, with the 78th Company, Sixth Marines. In early June he hardened to combat as the regiment smashed some of the best German troops at Chateau-Thierry, Bouresches, and nearby Belleau Wood.

Pruitt had one weakness — impatience. Whenever the regiment started toward the German lines, he had a tendency to get well out in front of his company, impatient to get at the enemy. This habit nearly cost him his life 14 June 1918, when he hurried on ahead of the company into an area polluted with poison gas. Pruitt dropped to the ground with his lungs on fire and sucking for breath. This warned the company from getting caught in the gas, but it put Pruitt in the hospital for five weeks.

Returning to the regiment 23 July 1918, Pruitt was promoted to corporal three weeks later.

In the closing stages of the war, the French Army finally gave up trying to take a German strongpoint at Blanc Mont Ridge. The Sixth Marines volunteered to tackle the fortified ridgetop, arriving in position 2 October 1918. They drove some German snipers out of a network of trenches, in order to get a good jump-off point for the assault the next day.

Dawn found Pruitt roving about the trenches, impatient to get moving. Higher strategy didn't concern him, but he had overheard enough to know the importance of the ridge that lay a couple of miles to the north, a ridge that was the key to the German defense for the entire section. If the regiment could overrun that position, they would force a major German pull-back.

Pruitt studied the open area the Marines would have to cross, between a small forested area on the right and a long trench atop a hill on the left. Even getting to the base of Blanc Mont Ridge would be tough, but with the confidence of a young Marine he knew they would succeed in hours where the French had failed for years.

Two hundred artillery pieces opened up at 5:50 a.m., pounding the distant ridge and German positions on the near side. Five minutes later, the Marines went over the top, with the artillery keeping a rolling barrage just ahead of them. Heavy fire poured out of the German outposts immediately, and soon from the main position on the ridgetop.

Pruitt skirted around the end of one barbed-wire entanglement which still held several blue clad bodies of French soldiers who had tried earlier to crack the German strongpoint. He hurried his squad on past the bodies.

When the Marines drew closer to Blanc Mont Ridge, Corporal Pruitt once again began to pull away from the rest of his company. The others didn't move fast enough for an eager youngster whose 22nd birthday was just hours away. Pruitt was the first to start up the slope of the ridge itself. Here, entanglements of barbed wire slowed him, and fire from the network of trenches and concrete positions filled the air around him. But mere bullets couldn't penetrate the magic of eager young courage.

At one point on the slope, Pruitt charged a nest of two machine guns, firing his Springfield from the hip and killing both gunners. Behind the position he found a dugout where 40 Germans hid from the barrage, without realizing the devil dogs were already on them. Pruitt stepped into the entrance with rifle ready.

"Fight or surrender," Pruitt demanded. All 40 surrendered, marching out in single file.

The toughest fighting of the battle occurred along that slope. Later in the morning, Pruitt again moved out well ahead of his company, this time sniping at a machine gun nest he couldn't get to, a little above and to his right. He killed the gunner, then started forward just as an artillery shell exploded a few feet away. The shrapnel slashed and ripped through his body, killing him and hurling his body down the slope. His death spurred his buddies to greater effort, and before the day ended they routed the Germans from the ridge.

Pruitt received Medals of Honor from both the Army and the Navy for the events of the last day of his life. He also received the Silver Star, French Croix de Guerre, and Italian Cross of Military Valor, all posthumously. His body was brought back to the United States 4 October 1921, for burial in Arlington National Cemetery.

The Navy later named a destroyer for the spunky kid from Arkansas.

EIGHTEENTH DOUBLE WINNER John Pruitt.

CHAPTER NINETEEN

John Joseph Kelly
(1898-1957)

The last of the double winners of the Medal of Honor, probably the last for all time, was John Joseph Kelly, a rock-fisted little Irishman who enjoyed knuckle fighting as recreation.

Born 24 June 1898, in Chicago, Kelly "grew up rough" on Chicago's tough south side, despite his lack of size. When he enlisted in the U.S. Marines 15 May 1918, he stood only five feet five inches tall and weighed only 112 pounds. But when stirred up, and he often was, he was a real ball of fury.

Assigned to the 78th Company, Sixth Marines, 20 August 1917, Kelly landed in France the following February. His first "combat" was with a British soldier in an argument over the British "mistreatment of the Irish" in Ireland for the past century or so. This resulted in the first of several disciplinary actions against him for fighting.

The Sixth Marines occupied trenches in the Verdun sector from 15 March to 14 May 1918, with little action. Kelly, who looked even younger than his nineteen years, became the company runner, carrying messages to various units. He developed legendary speed, agility and courage in darting through battle areas.

Kelly's first chance at showing super courage came near Chateau-Thierry. Here, from 1 June to 14 July 1918, the Sixth Marines set up a line across the German road to Paris.

During one German attack, Kelly ran orders to an outlying company. On the way back he passed an old farm house and found a Marine with a leg blown off. He put a tourniquet on the stump and tried to lift the man on his back. But the Marine outweighed Kelly by nearly a hundred pounds. Kelly spotted a ladder near the old house and ran over to it, ignoring heavy German artillery fire. He dragged the ladder back to the wounded Marine, wrapped him in a poncho and rolled him over on the ladder. Lifting one end of the makeshift stretcher, Kelly started dragging it to an aide station.

Somehow the little guy struggled to safety with his burden, saving the man's life. For this he received the first of four citations equivalent to the Silver Star.

During a gas barrage 14 June, Kelly inhaled enough of the deadly fumes to knock him out of action briefly; but he shook it off and returned to his company.

Kelly received his second citation and a French Croix de Guerre during the heavy fighting of 25 June. The French award cited his "great courage . . . carrying orders to advanced positions under a violent fire of artillery and machine guns."

Four days later, 29 June 1918, a piece of shrapnel ripped through Kelly's thigh, sending him to a hospital near Bordeaux. He was lucky at that, since he was one of only 11 survivors in his platoon that day.

While the wound healed, Kelly visited Paris and didn't even get into enough of a fight to be arrested.

The Sixth Marines took their next lumps in the Saint Mihiel campaign 12-15 September 1918. After three days the Germans stopped the Americans on the side of a hill, then counterattacked with artillery and machine gun fire concentrated on Kelly's company. For hours Kelly ran his messages, while the Germans gradually whittled down the number of effectives in the company.

By late afternoon, all officers had been killed or severely wounded. Kelly searched through the trenches until he found a sergeant and told him he was the highest ranking of 20 Marines still able to fight. He and the sergeant launched a counterattack, the sergeant taking about half the men to the right and Kelly taking the others to the left.

Stumbling and crawling over the rough terrain, the Marines stirred up more return fire than they could handle. The two squads converged on a cluster of rocks, after losing six men. German fire barked at them from all directions now, showing they were surrounded and cut off.

Three times the Germans attacked the dwindling Marines. Kelly fed belts of ammunition into a machine gun, fired by a corporal during the first two attacks. Then a machine gun bullet had hit the corporal, draping him over his weapon. Kelly pushed the body to one side and began firing at the line of Germans, driving them off this second time.

A third assault also was repelled, but only eight Marines could still fight. During a fourth attack, reinforcements arrived in time to drive off the Germans.

Kelly then helped drag wounded Marines to safety. For the day's battle, he received his third citation.

The Second Division — including the Third Marines — relieved the French in the line near Somme Puy 1 October. French dead lay everywhere, rotting. The bodies had to be removed before the Marines could move around effectively.

Kelly ran messages all that first night, while a hidden German machine gun searched for targets in the Marine position. At dawn, Kelly — the smallest man in the outfit — led two lieutenants and a corporal crawling along the network of trenches seeking the machine gun. Each time he reached a bend in the trench, Kelly carefully peeked around the corner. Seeing nothing, he crawled on to the next turn, followed by the other three.

Finally, he peeked around a bend and found piles of French dead, the stench of which nearly gagged him. The machine gun had to be just ahead. He moved just enough to spot a pillbox at the far end of the trench, then pulled back and whispered his findings to the others.

Then Kelly led them up and out of the trench, across the open area to a spot behind the pillbox. The four of them then charged from the blind side and ran upon the pillbox. Kelly dropped a grenade down the air vent, killing the Germans inside.

Kelly's finest moment came the following day, 3 October, when the Marines charged uphill toward Blanc Mont Ridge until a machine gun stopped them. The Marine commander then called for a barrage on the ridge.

While the big shells pounded the ridge, Kelly grabbed a grenade and pulled the pin, but kept the lever pressed down so the timing mechanism would not start ticking off the seconds to explosion. Then he pulled his 45 caliber pistol with his left hand and cocked it. Stand back, Krauts, here comes Kelly.

The other Marines didn't believe their eyes were working properly when they saw Kelly charge directly into the American barrage and smoke. Even more difficult to believe, he survived while running a full hundred yards toward the German position.

Then Kelly spotted a German running toward him. He aimed his pistol at the soldier, who promptly discarded his rifle, raised his hands and began to tearfully beg for his life.

Kelly hesitated, which likely saved his life because the

German then turned his head to the right. Kelly followed his glance, and through the smoke he spotted a large shellhole, hiding the machine gun that had stopped the company. The gunner trained the weapon around to fire at him and Kelly shot him, dropped to his left knee and hurled the grenade. A second gunner grabbed the machine gun, but the grenade exploded, killing him and those closest to him.

Eight other Germans came up out of the shellhole with hands raised over their heads. Kelly marched them and his other prisoner through the barrage back to his own lines.

For the day's fighting, Kelly received Medals of Honor from both the Army and Navy, the French Croix de Guerre with palm and the Medaille Militaire, the Italian Merito di Guerre and Montenegrin War Cross, and his fourth citation.

Kelly's outfit spent the final 11 days of the war in the Meuse-Argonne offensive. During the course of the battle, Kelly strayed over into the area of an adjoining division, where he and others were pinned down for about 45 minutes. Then Kelly took over an American machine gun and knocked out the German weapon. He then led an attack on the wooded area behind the gun emplacement, found a dugout and lobbed a grenade inside. The moment it exploded, Kelly charged inside where he found one dead and seven wounded Germans.

For this stunt Kelly receive his fifth citation. The Germans surrendered 11 November 1918.

Kelly later marched with the allied armies through Belgium and Luxembourg to the Rhine. He served with the army of occupation 13 December 1918 — 15 March 1919, during which General Pershing decorated him with his Army Medal of Honor, the Navy Cross and the Belguim Cross, and offered him a commission, which he refused.

Kelly was discharged 14 August 1919, at Quantico, Virginia. He later claimed he received less than one dollar for eight months combat pay, due to fines for fighting.

After separation, Kelly drifted around, mostly in Illinois and Florida, drinking too much to find anything permanent to do with his life. He didn't marry.

Death came 20 November 1957, in Florida, with burial in Des Plaines, Illinois.

National Archives

NINETEENTH DOUBLE WINNER John Joseph Kelly.

EPILOGUE

Perhaps the most amazing fact about the double winners of the Medal of Honor is that not one of them is well known today, and only three — Tom Custer, Dan Daly and Smedley Butler — were famous in their own time. Some recognition was accorded them — destroyers were named for Daly, Butler and Pruitt, and a small army camp named for Patrick Leonard — but, today, the general public couldn't name a single double winner.

The only bond common to all the 19 men was that each showed exceptional courage under fire. Also significant is the fact that 14 of the 19 were career servicemen. They came from a broad cross-section of American life, of varied national origins, religions, economic, cultural and educational levels. Five were natives of Ireland, two of Austria, one each of Norway and the West Indies. The ten American native sons included three from New York, two from Ohio, and one each from Michigan, Pennsylvania, Arkansas, Illinois and Louisiana. One was Black and 18 were Caucasian.

One widely accepted myth is that Medal of Honor winners usually paid for their decorations with their lives. This certainly was not true of the double winners. Only 3 of 19 were killed in action, only one while earning the medal.

None of the 19 was large physically, and 7 were considered undersized.

Personalities ranged from the boastful, arrogant Tom

Custer to the quiet, hard-boiled Dan Daly; from the colorless, steady and reliable Frank Baldwin to the flamboyant Smedley Butler; with ages ranging from the 19-year-old Tom Custer to the 44-year-old John King.

Not one of the double winners was a brutal or vicious person, though all were exceptionally tough when the occasion demanded it. The highest ranking double winner, Butler, was a major at the time he earned his second award.

In this era of downgrading America and her heroes, it is fashionable to claim that medal winners were people who cared little for their own lives because of their environments — that they had nothing to lose or to live for. None of the double winners match this description. Rather, all possessed a zest for life and a dedication to military service and America.

355.1342 Tassin C. 1
Tassin, Ray.
Double winners of the medal
of honor

OM 8-29-91 BKM 1-11-93
OS 9-30-91
ST 10-31-91 PL Keep
TC 4-23-92
ET 5-21-92
WH 9-10-92
AG 10-16-93

Iosco-Arenac Regional Library,
Tawas City, Michigan